engage

D1078812

Diversity. That's the best way to sum up issue 16 of engage. From the story of a Jewish beauty queen to Jesus' death on the cross. From Ezekiel's wild visions to James' practical advice on Christian living. There's something for everyone so jump right in.

[*] DAILY READINGS Each day's page throws you into the Bible, to get you handling, questioning and exploring God's message to you — encouraging you to act on it and talk to God more in prayer.

THIS ISSUE: Experience incredible visions with **Ezekiel;** be challenged and encouraged by **James;** meet **Esther,** God's beauty queen; and follow Jesus' call to get ready in **Matthew.**

[*] TAKE IT FURTHER If you're hungry for more at the end of an engage page, turn to the **Take it further** section to dig deeper.

[*] STUFF Articles on stuff relevant to the lives of young Christians. This issue: **self-harm and eating disorders.**

[*] TRICKY tackles those mind-bendingly tricky questions that confuse us all, as well as questions our friends bombard us with. This time we ask: **What's the meaning of life?**

[*] REAL LIVES True stories, revealing God at work in people's lives. This time — **we meet Anand, who was brought up as a Hindu.**

[*] ESSENTIAL Articles on the basics we really need to know about God, the Bible and Christianity. This issue, we find out exactly what **church** is.

[*] TOOLBOX is full of tools to help you understand the Bible. This issue we concentrate on **quotations in the Bible.**

All of us who work on engage are passionate to see the Bible at work in people's lives. Do you want God's word to have an impact on your life? Then open your Bible, and start on the first engage study right now...

1 Set a time you can read the Bible every day

2 Find a place where you can be quiet and think

3 Grab your Bible, pen and a notebook

4 Ask God to help you understand what you read

5 Read the day's verses with **engage**, taking time to think about it

6 Pray about what you've read

BIBLE STUFF We use the NIV Bible version, so you might find it's the best one to use with **engage**. If the notes say **"Read Ezekiel 1 v 1–3"**, look up Ezekiel in the contents page at the front of your Bible. It'll tell you which page Ezekiel starts on. Find chapter 1 of Ezekiel, and then verse 1 of chapter 1 (the verse numbers are the tiny ones). Then start reading. Simple.

In this issue...

ENGAGE 16 IS BROUGHT TO YOU BY THE DIVERSE TEAM OF...

Writers: Martin "scruffy" Cole   Carl "posh shoes" Laferton
          Helen "rabbit lover" Thorne   Cassie "nice hair" Martin
Designer: The wise, mature (and elderly) Steve Devane
Proof-readers Anne Woodcock from England   Nicole Carter from the USA
Editor: Martin Cole from the planet Piffle (martin@thegoodbook.co.uk)

EKEKIEL

Know God, know hope

Let's dive straight into the jaw-dropping book of Ezekiel. It's er... Well, the book kind of... Um... We're lost for words. Ezekiel left us terrified, overwhelmed, humbled, shocked and full of hope — all at the same time.

It could make you a different person too. In a mix of visions, drama, parables and poetry, Ezekiel blows apart any cosy, easy-to-contain, know-it-all view of God.

Ezekiel comes near the end of the Old Testament period. It's set in the last days of the tiny nation of Judah and its capital, Jerusalem. All that's left of the once great nation of Israel. In 597BC, armies from Babylon, sent by God, besieged Jerusalem and took the king (and several thousand others) into exile in Babylon. Including the prophet Ezekiel.

In 587BC, Judah collapsed. God was bringing His judgment so that His people would realise who He really is. The Babyonian troops pulverised Jerusalem and its temple, the very place where God had shared His presence with His people.

God called Ezekiel to start preaching in 593BC — a few years before Jerusalem was completely conquered. Ezekiel spoke to a people under God's judgment. Just like the world today. People live, most not realising it, with God against them, facing His punishment for the way they've treated Him.

And what's God's message to people in that situation? First, it's a message of no hope. Once people realise there is no hope in a life rejecting God, they can discover that there is real hope for those who know God and His Son, Jesus.

Know God, as He really is, and know hope.

1 | Tell a vision

Ezekiel's book is eye-opening and mind-blowing, right from the start. Get ready for visions of God. Watch out for violent storms, weird creatures, lots of fire and something even more spectacular.

👁 Read Ezekiel 1 v 1–3

ENGAGE YOUR BRAIN

▶ What happened to Ezekiel when he was 30? (v1, 3)

Ezekiel switched from redundant priest (far from the Jerusalem temple) to red-hot prophet. God would speak again to His people — even far away in Babylon.

👁 Read verses 4–21

▶ What did Ezekiel see in his vision? (v4–9)

▶ How are the creatures described? (v10–14)

▶ What else did Ezekiel see? (v15, 21)

These four amazing creatures, with all their faces and wings, could see and move in any direction. Next to the creatures were incredible wheels/chariots that could move "wherever the Spirit [God's Spirit] would go"

(v20). But Ezekiel was about to see something even more amazing.

👁 Read verses 22–28

▶ What incredible, terrifying thing did Ezekiel see next? (v22–24)

▶ Who did Ezekiel see and how was he described? (v26–28)

The four creatures carried a vast platform. On it, seated on a throne, was an amazing fiery figure. This appears to be a glimpse of God Himself in human form — Jesus Christ. The book of Ezekiel is about God's message to His people and it keeps pointing to the coming of Jesus. Tomorrow we'll find out what the voice said to Ezekiel.

PRAY ABOUT IT

What is it about God that should leave you amazed? Praise and thank your all-powerful God right now.

→ TAKE IT FURTHER

Ezekiel basics on page 109.

2 | Mission impossible?

Ezekiel is having a vision of God and he's already seen some spectacular things. Now God tells Ezekiel exactly what his mission is. It's not going to be an easy one.

👁 Read Ezekiel 2 v 1–8

ENGAGE YOUR BRAIN

▶ *What was Ezekiel's mission? (v3)*

▶ *What hazards would he face? (v4–7)*

▶ *How must Ezekiel be different? (v8)*

👁 Read Ezekiel 2 v 9 – 3 v 15

▶ *How did God give Ezekiel the words to say? (v1–4)*

▶ *Why would it be a difficult mission? (v7)*

▶ *How would God help Ezekiel cope with opposition? (v8–9)*

Ezekiel's task was to take God's words of coming judgment to a people with a history of walking out on God and snubbing His spokesmen. No easy job, and one that scared Ezekiel.

👁 Read verss 16–27

▶ *What made Ezekiel's mission so vital? (18–21)*

▶ *What was the first surprising stage of his mission? (v24–27)*

God's message to His people was this — turn back to me or face the terrible consequences. It was Ezekiel's mission to deliver this message. By warnings and judgment, God's people would have to learn that God ruled. He's in control and He won't be upstaged.

PRAY ABOUT IT

Do you still think of yourself as centre of the universe? Ask the Lord to use Ezekiel to give you a clear perspective on life, with God at the centre of it.

→ TAKE IT FURTHER

Find a little bit more on page 109.

3 | Siege mentality

Ezekiel's first task was to preach about the future of God's city, Jerusalem. He'd show what would happen to the city by lying outside for a year, making models and cooking food on burning poo. Yes, really.

👁 Read Ezekiel 4 v 1–8

ENGAGE YOUR BRAIN

▶ How did Ezekiel show what would happen to Jerusalem? (v1–3)

▶ What would this reveal about God's people? (v4, 6)

The Israelites had sinned against God for many years and would be punished for it. God told Ezekiel to lie on his side and "put the sin of the house of Israel" on himself (v4). This points us forward to Jesus who would suffer and die for peple's sin.

👁 Read verses 9–17

▶ What else did God tell Ezekiel to do? (v9–12)

▶ What did this symbolise? (v13, 16–17)

Cooking with dung is disgusting but it's nothing compared to what would happen to Jerusalem. God's people would be attacked and they'd suffer a famine. But their real famine would be a spiritual one.

THINK IT OVER

▶ How seriously does God treat sin?

▶ How will He treat those who reject Him?

▶ How should that affect our relationships with non-Christians?

▶ What are our responsibilities?

PRAY ABOUT IT

Pray for people you know who are "spiritually starving". Ask God to feed them with the bread of life.

THE BOTTOM LINE

Spiritual famine is deadly.

→ TAKE IT FURTHER

More about the bread of life on page 109.

4 | Hairy story

Ezekiel is lying outside for over a year with a model of Jerusalem to illustrate what will happen to the city. And Ezekiel's not finished yet. Time for a shave...

👁 Read Ezekiel 5 v 1–17

ENGAGE YOUR BRAIN
- ▶ What did God tell Ezekiel to do next? (v1–4)
- ▶ What could the people of Jerusalem expect? (v2, 4)
- ▶ Why? (v5–6)
- ▶ How bad were God's people? (v7)
- ▶ What specifically had they done wrong? (v9)
- ▶ What would happen to them?
  v10:
  v11:
  v12:
- ▶ What effect would this have?
  v13:
  v15:

Imagine using a sword to shave your head — tricky! Ezekiel performed all these signs to show how devastating God's punishment would be. A third of the people would die from disease; a third would be killed by the sword; and a third would be exiled — sent to a foreign country.

This all sounds harsh (especially the cannibalism) but this was God's special, chosen people. He'd done so many incredible things for them and forgiven them so many times. Yet they continued to sin against Him and worship other gods. Unparalleled sin required unheard-of punishment. They got what they deserved.

THINK IT OVER
- ▶ Why do we sometimes gloss over this side of God's character?
- ▶ What should God's anger remind us about sin?
- ▶ How should it affect the way we live?

PRAY ABOUT IT
Ask God to give you a true perspective on sin and how much it offends Him. Spend time talking to God about sins you struggle with, asking Him for help.

→ TAKE IT FURTHER
Hairy history on page 109.

5 : Idol speculation

Things were looking bleak for Jerusalem. Surely it's time for some hope. Er, not yet (though it will come later in Ezekiel, we promise!). Now the target for God's punishment gets bigger than just Jerusalem.

👁 Read Ezekiel 6 v 1–14

ENGAGE YOUR BRAIN

▷ *What would God do because His people worshipped idols instead of Him? (v4–6)*

▷ *What would it achieve? (v7)*

▷ *What hope was there? (v8)*

▷ *What happens when people realise how badly they've treated God? (v9)*

▷ *What would happen to Israel? (v11–14)*

👁 Skim read Ezekiel 7 v 1–27

▷ *What new message did Ezekiel bring? (v2, 3, 6)*

▷ *What had made this judgment unstoppable? (v8–9)*

▷ *What must these idol worshippers realise? (v4, 9, 27)*

It was one thing to say God would act in judgment. Quite another to say God was now on His way. Frightening. Maybe Ezekiel's hearers hoped for a quick return to Jerusalem. Ezekiel was saying: "You ain't seen nothing yet". No God, no hope.

THINK IT OVER

▷ *What false hopes about God do people cling to today?*

▷ *What do these chapters force us to see about God?*

PRAY ABOUT IT

Thank God that He deals with sin and treats everyone fairly. Thank Him that, despite our sin, He sent Jesus to deal with our disgusting sin problem.

→ TAKE IT FURTHER

Idol talk on page 110.

6 | Idol talk

The end was definitely on its way for Jerusalem. Next, God gave Ezekiel a supernatural bird's-eye view of its destruction. You may find some scenes quite disturbing. Ezekiel did.

👁 Read Ezekiel 8 v 1–16

ENGAGE YOUR BRAIN

▶ What did Ezekiel see in this new vision? (v2–4)

▶ What "detestable" stuff did he see happening in Jerusalem?
v5–6:
v7–13:
v16:

Shocking. In God's temple in God's city, idols were being worshipped instead of God. You can probably guess what God's response will be.

Read 8 v 17 – 9 v 11

▶ What are the answers to God's questions in v17?

▶ What shows us it's too late for God's people? (v18)

▶ Who did the man with the writing kit save? (v4)

▶ What happened to everyone else? (v5–6)

▶ What upset Ezekiel? (v8)

▶ What was God's answer? (v9–10)

God's pitiless judgment would start with individuals (ch 9) and then reach the whole city (chs 10-11). But there was a glimmer of hope — those who were upset by all the sin against God would be saved. So far, this book seems heartless, cruel and depressing. But we will see God's great love and compassion shining through.

THINK IT OVER

▶ What would you say to someone who suggested it doesn't matter which god you worship?

PRAY ABOUT IT

Pray for friends of other faiths. Pray that God would show them He's the one true God.

THE BOTTOM LINE

Don't worship anything other than God. He won't tolerate it.

→ TAKE IT FURTHER

More talk on page 110.

7 | God's gone

We're inside another of Ezekiel's terrifying visions. Remember the four creatures from earlier? The ones with four faces and four wings and weird wheel things? Well, they're here too and they're called cherubim.

👁 Read Ezekiel 10 v 1–17

ENGAGE YOUR BRAIN

▶ *What new task was the writing kit guy given? (v2, 6–7)*

▶ *Whose presence was still in the temple? (v4)*

In his vision, Ezekiel saw God on a sapphire throne. The Lord sent a man to scatter hot coals over Jerusalem — to destroy it. Even worse than that, God was on the move...

👁 Read verses 18–22

▶ *What dreadful thing happened? (v18)*

God was about to remove Himself from His city — to abandon it. This was far worse than any of the punishments so far. Being abandoned by God is the worse thing that can happen to anyone. But it's the punishment for anyone who constantly rejects the Lord.

God's people had finished with Him. They refused to turn back to Him. So, eventually, God's patience ran out and He finished with them. They got what they asked for.

And yet that wasn't the end of the story for God's people. A small remnant would be saved. Tomorrow, Ezekiel will actually give us a message of hope! Really.

PRAY ABOUT IT

Rejecting God and being abandoned by Him is deadly serious. If you mean it, tell God you're committed to Him and ask Him never to leave you.

Pray for people you know who refuse to turn to God. However unlikely it seems, pray that God will do something miraculous in their lives.

→ TAKE IT FURTHER

Going going gone... to page 110.

8 | A new hope

Ezekiel is packed full of doom and gloom and nothing else. Right? Wrong! Today we see great hope for God's people. OK, so maybe a little bit of doom and gloom first...

👁 Read Ezekiel 11 v 1–12

ENGAGE YOUR BRAIN

▷ *What were the leaders of Jerusalem doing? (v2)*

▷ *What did they claim? (v3)*

▷ *What would happen to those arrogant murderers? (v9–10)*

▷ *What would they realise? (v12)*

The evil leaders of Jerusalem were so arrogant: "We're safe on the inside, like meat in a pot." Oh no they're not. There was no hope for them once they'd rejected God.

👁 Read verses 13–25

▷ *What was Ezekiel worried about? (v13)*

▷ *How did God comfort Him? (v16–17)*

▷ *What would God's people do?*
v18:
v19:
v20:

Ezekiel gets great news at last! God would take some of His faithful people back to His city. Check out the book of Nehemiah to see how this happened.

But Ezekiel is also pointing us to further into the future. Because of Jesus' death and resurrection, God's people will have a perfect future with Him. He will "put a new spirit" in His people (v19). They will be His people and He will be their God (v20). Forever. That's the brilliant future for all believers.

PRAY ABOUT IT

Do you look forward to your eternal future? Thank God for His promises. Thank Him that He will never leave those who trust in Him. Thank Him for the hope of a perfect future.

→ TAKE IT FURTHER

No *Take it furthe*r today.

9 ┊ A big breakthrough ┊

God keeps asking Ezekiel to do some weird stuff — they're pictures of what would happen to God's people. This time it involves a little domestic destruction.

👁 Read Ezekiel 12 v 1–16

ENGAGE YOUR BRAIN

▶ *What did God tell Ezekiel to do? (v3–6)*

▶ *What did it symbolise? (v10–14)*

▶ *Would anyone listen? (v2)*

▶ *What would they realise when it all came true? (v15–16)*

Only 4 years later, this all happened (2 Kings 25). Zedekiah tried to escape late at night but the Babylonians captured him. They took him back to Babylon, where he was executed.

👁 Read verses 17–28

▶ *Why would the people be anxious? (v19–20)*

▶ *Yet what was their attitude? (v22, 27)*

▶ *What was God's answer to them? (v23–25)*

People either said Ezekiel's words were nonsense and never came true, or they said: "Don't worry — none of this will happen for years". Both were dead wrong. God *would* punish this rebellious nation — and very soon.

Many people think Christianity is a load of rubbish and reject it. Others understand the gospel message but put off doing anything about it. For now they'll carry on living for themselves. But Jesus could return anytime. Don't leave it too late. It *will* happen. God's enemies *will* be punished and only believers saved.

SHARE IT

Think of someone you know who thinks Christianity is nonsense. And someone who knows the gospel but refuses to let it affect the way they live. Think of how you can share the truth of Jesus with these two people. Pray for them every day this week.

→ TAKE IT FURTHER

Another breakthrough on page 110.

10 Prophet and loss

Well done for sticking with us through this challenging book. Just one more section to go before you get a breather and some practical tips for Christian living from James. But first, one more hard-hitting blast of Ezekiel.

👁 Read Ezekiel 13 v 1–16

ENGAGE YOUR BRAIN
▷ *Why were these false prophets so dangerous? (v2–3, 6)*

These teachers were like builders who try to hide defects in a building with a bit of white paint. What appears to be a normal, strong building could come crashing down at any moment. If people wanted to hear a message of peace, then that's what these false prophets would give them. But soon they'd feel the full force of God's anger against those who reject Him.

👁 Read verses 17–23
▷ *How were these women deceiving people? (v18)*
▷ *What was God's message to them? (v20–23)*

👁 Read Ezekiel 14 v 1–11
▷ *Why would God punish idol worshippers? (v5)*
▷ *What must anyone do who worships other gods? (v6)*

👁 Read verses 12–23
▷ *"Jerusalem will survive — a few godly people are left." How did God answer this claim? (v13–14)*
▷ *Why would some sinful people survive? (v22–23)*

The people of Jerusalem thought they were invincible — they were God's chosen people. But the hard truth is that *anyone* who turns away from God can expect to face the fierce consequences. Ever think you'll be fine because you go to church or are from a Christian family? Or because you're not as bad as some people you know? You'll only be eternally safe if you trust in Jesus' death for you and live your life for Him.

PRAY ABOUT IT
Pray that you won't be fooled by false teaching. Thank God for giving all Christians the Holy Spirit to help them to live His way and trust His promises.

→ TAKE IT FURTHER
A tiny bit more on page 111.

The meaning of life

Each issue in TRICKY, we tackle those mind-bendingly difficult questions that confuse us all, as well as questions that friends bombard us with to catch us out. This time: **What's the meaning of life?**

This is a huge question and one that people have been asking for as long as they've been around. Depending on who you ask, you might get the answer: "To be happy"; "To have as much fun as you can before you die"; or, if your friend is a Sci-Fi geek, then maybe their answer will be "42".

MEANINGLESS?

But what does the Bible say the meaning of life is? What does God tell us? Well, one good place to look is at the book of Ecclesiastes. Despite its depressing refrain of *"Meaningless, meaningless, everything is meaningless"* (Ecclesiastes 1 v 2 etc), this book of the Bible is all about the meaning of life.

The writer (probably King Solomon) tries to find meaning in learning and education, pleasure and fun, riches and possessions, hard work and success, but ultimately finds them all "meaningless". Have a read through the book if you haven't already — his search for meaning is still massively relevant today.

MEANINGFUL RELATIONSHIPS

Surprisingly, the conclusion that Ecclesiastes reaches is that life does have meaning but only because one day God will judge the world. A strange reason you might think, but it shows us that our life here and now matters. God cares about what we do and the choices we make, and will hold us accountable. Our lives matter; they have meaning.

So what is the meaning of life, according to Ecclesiastes? Chapter 12, verse 1 tells us to *"remember your creator in the days of your youth"*.

Remember God now. He should be at the centre of your life, because He gave it to you and He will judge how you've used that life.

So the meaning of life is to live in relationship with God — giving Him thanks and living to please Him.

THE MEANING OF LIFE

Problem: we don't naturally live in thankfulness to God, nor do we remember Him. We're like a malfunctioning machine that isn't doing the task for which it was made. But Jesus came to repair us. In John 10 v 10–11, Jesus tells us that He has come to die so that we may have *"life to the full"*. Jesus' perfect life — full of truth and meaning and in perfect relationship with His Father — can be ours if we trust in what Jesus did on the cross.

The Bible tells us that God is love (1 John 4 v 8). God didn't create us because He was lonely and needed someone to have a relationship with. God is a Trinity — Father, Son and Holy Spirit living in perfect loving relationship. God is love. And He wants to share that love. By creating us and saving us, it shows His love and brings Him great glory.

A group of Christians way back in the 17th century summarised the meaning of life like this: "The chief end of man [i.e. the reason for which we were created] is to glorify God and enjoy Him forever".

By enjoying God's love, by thanking Him for creating and saving us, by living for Him and delighting in His presence and care every day, we glorify Him. That is what we were made for. That is the meaning of life, now and forever.

James

Fantastic faith

Are you ready for some practical training in living as a Christian? Then James is the book for you.

Whether you have trouble with temptation, showing favouritism or letting your words upset people, James has advice for you. There's also instruction on putting your faith into action and not joining in with the world's ways. Vital stuff.

James was a brother of Jesus and leader of the church in Jerusalem. He wrote this letter about 20 years after Jesus' death and resurrection. Its written to Jews who had become Christians. These guys had been persecuted and scattered all over.

These Christians seemed to be arguing loads and the church was in danger of tearing itself apart. A drought wasn't helping things either. Farmers with no crops and no money were being exploited by rich businessmen — and all were members of the same church. Ouch.

Pressure and persecution from outside the church was causing stress too. Other problems included rich Christians assuming they were more important than everyone else; people causing offence with their pride, gossiping and harsh words; and believers struggling with temptation.

This letter is full of wise words to all of those people and to us, too, who fight the same battles and temptations. James tells us loads about what God is like and how we must work at a right relationship with Him. And with each other as well.

James has words to challenge and encourage all believers. So listen up and make sure you act on what God teaches you through this great letter.

11 ┆ James on trial

What's your usual response when life is hard? And when you're hassled for being a Christian? James says: Celebrate! Enjoy it! Surely he's a little confused...

👁 **Read James 1 v 1-4**

ENGAGE YOUR BRAIN

▶ *What's so good about tough times testing your faith? (v3)*

▶ *And what's the end result? (v4)*

OK, so we may feel really low when we face trials in life... but we're to consider them "pure joy". James tells us to remember that God uses tough times to build us up. Our faith grows and we learn to persevere — stick at being a Christian. And as we stick at it, we'll grow in maturity as believers.

In heaven, the work of God making us more like Jesus will be completed. We'll be like Him. What a future!

👁 **Read verses 5-8**

Wisdom doesn't mean being great at school/college or anything like that. True wisdom is knowing how to live God's way.

▶ *How do we get wisdom? (v5)*

▶ *What does God promise? (v5)*

▶ *What else is required of us? (v6)*

If we ask God, He'll make us wise and help us to live for Him. We must trust God to be true to His generous character. If we don't, James says we're "double-minded" — in two minds, with split loyalties — and so unlikely to make any progress in faith.

PRAY ABOUT IT

Talk to God about anything you need to change. Maybe your attitude? Ask Him to help you survive the trials of life so that you increase in maturity, faith, wisdom and joy.

→ **TAKE IT FURTHER**

Follow the trial trail to page 111.

12 ┊ Cash or crown?

Many people chase after wealth, believing money can give them a good life and lead to happiness. But what are the true blessings from God that give meaning to life? And where can we find them?

👁 Read James 1 v 9–11

ENGAGE YOUR BRAIN

▶ *What's the surprising news for poor and rich people?*

▶ *What do you think James means?*

James has been talking about the trials Christians face in life (v2). Believers with little money obviously face tough times, trying to make ends meet. But rich Christians have it hard too — so many temptations that could lead them away from God. And wealth often doesn't last — loss of money brings trials too.

But both rich and poor Christians should be joyful about their situations, even when life is hard. We shouldn't view life using the world's standards, where having money is seen as success. So what's true success in God's eyes?

👁 Read verse 12

▶ *Who receives God's blessing?*

▶ *What will such believers receive?*

Life will be hard for Christians. But stick at it — it will be more than worth it. Those who persevere and don't turn away from God will receive the "crown of life". This is the gift God will give to all Christians. The brilliant and everlasting gift of eternal life from the King of kings to His faithful servants.

PRAY ABOUT IT

Pray for both rich and poor Christians you know. Pray that God will help them through the different trials they face, so that they rejoice and keep living for God.

THE BOTTOM LINE

"Blessed is the man who perseveres under trial, because when he has stood the test, he will receive the crown of life that God has promised to those who love him."

→ TAKE IT FURTHER

Run for the prize, to page 111.

13 | Tempting times

Sometimes, the trials of life can get very ugly. They can make us feel as if we're drowning and we become desperate for relief. That's when the easy way out looks very tempting.

👁 Read James 1 v 13–16

ENGAGE YOUR BRAIN

▶ What can lead us away from God? (v14)

▶ What mistake might we make when we're tempted to sin? (v13)

▶ Why is giving in to temptation so serious?

Sin separates us from God. And it's either punished or forgiven. Don't be deceived (v16). Acknowledge what you're like inside. But how can we keep going with God, when we're like this?

👁 Read verse 17–18

▶ Where do all good things come from? (v17)

▶ How is God described in v17?

▶ What does He do for all Christians? (v18)

God is in complete control. He created the whole universe, including the stars ("heavenly lights"). But, unlike them, He doesn't change and so is totally trustable. He's incredibly generous and has given us new birth. A new life. A fresh start. With His life in us, we can stick at living for Him. We can fight temptation.

THINK IT OVER

▶ What temptations do you face?

▶ How can your faith in God help you fight temptation?

PRAY ABOUT IT

Talk to God about any temptations you struggle with, asking Him to help you fight them. Thank Him that He's in control and that He will always give you strength to resist.

➔ TAKE IT FURTHER

Loads more on page 111.

14 ┊ Listen up ┊

**We've been given new life by God. Result.
Now James is going to tell us how we should
live that out. For starters, just calm down, will you??**

👁 Read James 1 v 19–20

ENGAGE YOUR BRAIN
▶ *What two pieces of advice does James give us in v19?*

▶ *Why is anger a problem? (v20)*

Great advice for all of us — take more time to listen. Listen to each other rather than doing all the talking. Or jumping into arguments. And listen to what God's teaching you in the Bible.

THINK IT OVER
▶ *How much do you listen to others in normal conversation?*

▶ *How are you at listening (and responding) to God's word?*

If we listen more than we talk, we'll see situations from other people's perspectives. And we'll be less likely to get angry with them. Likewise, if we take more time to listen to God's word, we'll be more likely to live His way.

We must do everything we can to avoid getting angry and being nasty with people. Anger gets in the way of righteousness — right living that pleases God.

GET ON WITH IT
▶ *When God's word challenges you, do you get angry, get defensive, start making excuses for yourself?*

▶ *Do you lose your temper? Why?*

▶ *How will you live "the righteous life that God desires" better?*

PRAY ABOUT IT
You know what you need to say to God today.

TAKE IT FURTHER
Oi, angrypants, go to page 111!

15 Mirror mirror on the wall

More top advice on how to live as a Christian. James has told us to be quick to listen, slow to speak and slow to get angry. So, what next?

👁 Read James 1 v 21

ENGAGE YOUR BRAIN

▷ *What two things are we told to do?*

▷ *What moral filth and evil do you need to throw out of your life?*

▷ *What part of God's word do you need to accept and take seriously?*

God's word has been planted in us. So let it grow by obedience to God and a ruthlessness with the wrong in our lives.

👁 Read verses 22–25

▷ *When we hear or read God's word, what must we do? (v22)*

▷ *Why? (v25)*

It's not enough to turn up at church or to read your Bible. It's pointless if you don't do what it says. It's like looking in a mirror and forgetting what you look like. When we dive into the Bible, we should expect to find out more about ourselves, about God and how He wants us to live. We need to remember what we've learned and then put it into action.

GET ON WITH IT

▷ *What action do you need to take?*

Try writing out what you've decided to do. Or copy out a relevant Bible verse. Then stick it to your mirror to remind you to do what God says. Verse 22 would be a good one to use.

THE BOTTOM LINE

Do not merely listen to the word, and so deceive yourselves. Do what it says.

→ TAKE IT FURTHER

Loads about law and freedom on page 111.

16 | Religious education

Would you call yourself religious?
Do you know anyone who would say they were?
What does it mean to be religious?
What is true religion anyway?

Read James 1 v 26

ENGAGE YOUR BRAIN
- *What kind of person isn't as religious as they claim to be?*

It's easy to claim to be a Christian or to be religious. But the things we say and do often show what we're really like. It's no good claiming to be a Christian if your words regularly let you down or upset people. We're deceiving ourselves.

GET ON WITH IT
- *In what ways do your words let yourself down and offend God?*

- *What will you do about it?*

Read verse 27
- *What two things here are accepted by God as true religion?*
  1.
  2.

"Widows and orphans" is Bible shorthand for those unable to give anything back in return for your help.

- *Do you mix with certain types of people and not others?*

- *Do you look after those people that others ignore?*

How do we stop ourselves "being polluted by the world"? We need to avoid being influenced negatively by society. Or by anyone who rejects God. So we're not led away from living for Him.

- *What ungodly influences are there in your life?*

- *How will you avoid being polluted by them?*

PRAY ABOUT IT
Look again at all today's questions. You should have loads to tell God and to ask Him for.

→ TAKE IT FURTHER
More education on page 112.

17 | Firm favourites

True religion starts with being born again. Then it's about trusting Jesus as we live His way. That will mean saying "Yes" to some things and a definite "No" to others. In the rest of his letter, James tells us what true religion is.

👁 Read James 2 v 1–4

ENGAGE YOUR BRAIN

▷ What are Christians told not to do? (v1)

▷ How was this happening in churches? (v2–3)

▷ What are we guilty of if we show favouritism? (v4)

👁 Read verse 5–7

▷ How does God often treat poorer people? (v5)

▷ But how were these Christians treating the poor? (v6)

▷ Yet what were some rich guys doing? (v6–7)

It's thought that, just to survive the drought, many farmers put themselves in major debt to the rich, who took them to court (v6) when they didn't keep up with payments. James says the rich shouldn't despise the poor. And the poor are to trust God, not look to the world to meet their needs.

Jesus didn't show favouritism — He often mixed with outsiders, those looked down on. He was treated as an outsider Himself and even died a criminal's death. We should care for the same sort of people Jesus did. And v5 tells us that God has chosen the poor, weak and insignificant to be "rich in faith". God often uses unlikely outsiders in His plans.

THINK IT OVER

Think how you judge people because of their: sex; colour; education; accent; politics; religious views; culture; interests; personal hygiene; nationality; popularity.

▷ Which prejudices do you need to confess to God right now?

→ TAKE IT FURTHER

Grab some more on page 112.

23

18 | Mercy side

Exciting times. Many Jews had trusted in Jesus and become Christians. Brilliant. But some had got muddled — thinking they had to follow Jesus AND keep the Old Testament Jewish law (sacrifices, circumcision etc).

👁 **Read James 2 v 8–11**

ENGAGE YOUR BRAIN

▶ *What was the "royal law"? (v8)*

▶ *What was the news for Christians who showed favouritism? (v9)*

▶ *How much of God's law do people need to keep to please God? (v10–11)*

These guys almost worshipped Jewish law. But James says it's impossible to keep it all. None of us can keep all of God's commands. Only trusting in Jesus can put us right with God.

James says to Christians: Don't live by the Jewish law, but by the gospel (the message of Jesus' death and resurrection). He calls the gospel "a law that gives freedom". That's what Jesus brings!

👁 **Read verses 12–13**

▶ *What's James' instruction? (v12)*

▶ *Why? (v13)*

We should be merciful (forgiving and compassionate) to people. Because God's shown great mercy to us. Even though we fail to keep His law, He sent His Son to take the punishment we deserve. That's real mercy. We should speak and act in a way that reflects God's mercy to us.

THINK IT OVER

▶ *Am I merciful to those who offend me?*

▶ *Am I compassionate with those in need (of any sort)?*

PRAY ABOUT IT

Ask God to help you trust in Jesus to put you right with Him, rather than relying on your own good behaviour. Ask Him to help you to show mercy and compassion to people you meet this week.

→ **TAKE IT FURTHER**

There's more on page 112.

19 | Faith in action

James didn't pull his punches. Many parts of his letter would have shocked its readers. He's already attacked "double-minded" believers, who say one thing but do another. Now he says faith without action is deadly.

Read James 2 v 14–19

ENGAGE YOUR BRAIN

▷ How would you answer v14?

▷ How does James answer it in v15–17?

▷ And in v18–19?

We've already seen that doing good things won't get you right with God. James *isn't* saying do good deeds to get to heaven. He's saying true faith is backed up by action. All talk and no action is no faith at all. We must show our faith by the way we live. Just believing that God exists isn't enough. Even demons do that (v19)!

Read verses 20–26

▷ What was Abraham prepared to do? (v21)

▷ What does this tell us about his faith in God?

▷ What does his example tell us about saving faith? (v24)

▷ What does Rahab's example tell us about saving faith? (v25–26)

Trusting God's promises, Abraham risked his son's death. God called him "righteous" — right with God. Justified (v24) means the same thing.

All talk and no action. All intellectual belief and no action. Such faith is no faith at all. A faith that saves is a faith that expresses itself in action. In self-sacrifice. In constant risk-taking trust.

THINK AND PRAY

▷ How much do you believe in God and actually live it out?

▷ Have a long, hard think and pray: is your faith living or dead?

→ TAKE IT FURTHER

Action stations on page 112.

20 Tongue twisting

Say this out loud: "She sells sea shells by the seashore". Now much faster. Sometimes it's hard to control your tongue. Tongue-twisters are one thing, but when our words offend people, that's much more serious.

👁 Read James 3 v 1

ENGAGE YOUR BRAIN

▶ What's James warning to people who want to be Bible teachers?

Some of those James was writing to probably thought they should be the ones doing the Bible teaching. Being accountable to God should make such people think twice: did they want such a role for their own ego or for others' good? James now describes why Bible teachers and all Christians need to be careful.

👁 Read verses 2–6

▶ Is anyone perfect in what they say? (v2)
▶ What is the tongue compared to?
▶ What huge effect can our words have on our lives? (v5–6)

If we manage to mostly control our tongues, it shows we have great self-control. But the person who lets their tongue run away with them is in danger of destruction (v6). If we don't control what we say, it can completely corrupt us.

👁 Read verses 7–12

▶ What's the warning in v8?
▶ How do our words show us to be double-minded? (v9–10)
▶ What's the point James makes in v11–12?

The tongue is uncontrollable (v8). We need God's help to tame it and not let our words run away from us. It's crazy to praise God at one moment and gossip about people the next.

THINK AND PRAY

▶ In what specific ways has your tongue taken over this week?
▶ Who have you offended or said nasty things about?
▶ What do you need to do about it?

Talk to God about these issues right now.

→ TAKE IT FURTHER

More tongue taming on page 112.

21 Wise up

Who's the wise one here? Angelica, who can predict the future of her business? Bob, who helps people tackle their problems? Cassie, an astro-physicist with a huge brain? Or Dan, who made up after an argement with a friend?

👁 Read James 3 v 13–16

ENGAGE YOUR BRAIN

▶ How is true wisdom shown? (v13)

▶ What's the definition of false wisdom? (v14)

▶ Where does it come from? (v15)

▶ What are its results? (v16)

Being wise, according to the world, is becoming a success; or being the best academically; or making heaps of money. James says that's not true wisdom. In fact, such "wisdom" is usually selfish, unspiritual and even comes from the devil. Such selfish ambition leads to disorders and sin.

👁 Read verses 17–18

▶ Where does true wisdom come from? (v17)

▶ What is it like? (v17)

▶ What's the great news for people who make peace? (v18)

True wisdom has less to do with knowledge or success, and more to do with attitude and behaviour. True wisdom is living to please God, not yourself.

GET ON WITH IT

▶ Read v17 again and pick two of these things you need to work harder at.

▶ What will you do exactly?

▶ Who do you need to make peace with?

PRAY ABOUT IT

Thank God that He's the source of true wisdom. Ask Him to help you grow in wisdom, especially improving on the areas you picked from v17. Pray that you'll be less selfish and better at peacemaking.

→ TAKE IT FURTHER

Keep the peace on page 113.

22 | Resistance is fertile

James is in doctor mode. His patient, the church, was seriously ill — it was proud, rude, selfish, and members showed no concern for each other. Some drastic surgery was needed before the church tore itself apart.

👁 Read James 4 v 1–3

ENGAGE YOUR BRAIN

▶ *What was the big problem in the church? (v1)*

▶ *What caused it and what were they failing to do? (v2)*

▶ *What was wrong with their praying? (v3)*

Envy and greed were causing huge arguments, messing up relationships in the church and with God. James' remedy: instead of being motivated by greed and selfishness, trust in God and care for others.

👁 Read verses 4–6

▶ *What's the truth for anyone who goes the world's way and lives to please themselves? (v4)*

▶ *What must we remember about God? (v5–6)*

We may have an inbuilt capacity for wrong (v5), but God gives all the help we need to resist it (v6). The only treatment is total repentance.

👁 Read verses 7–10

▶ *What's the great news for Christians when tempted by the devil? (v7)*

▶ *What does God expect us to do? (v8–10)*

▶ *What does He promise? (v8, 10)*

Do you envy other Christians' popularity, status or ability? Do you focus too much on possessions and money? Dr James says this is actually hatred of God that will choke our spiritual life. Humbly turning back to God is the only remedy.

PRAY ABOUT IT

Be openly honest with God. Re-read todays verses and talk to Him.

→ TAKE IT FURTHER

A tiny bit more is on page 113.

23 | Who's the judge?

Today James gives us more great advice for living the Christian life. The Christians he was writing to weren't living as God's people should. In fact, at times they were living as if He didn't exist.

Read James 4 v 11–12

ENGAGE YOUR BRAIN

- What's James' command in v11?
- Why shouldn't we say bad stuff about other Christians? (v11)
- Who's the only one who should judge people? (v12)

Some of these Christians thought they were better than others, and that thinking turned into words and criticism. That's slander. Anyone who slanders someone else is, in effect, judging God's law (which says, for example, "Love your neighbour as yourself"). The slanderer is saying: God's rules don't apply to me, so I'll say what I like. We all mess up and disobey God, so we're in no position to judge others. Leave that to God.

Read verses 13–17

- What attitude does James attack here? (v13)
- What's wrong with it? (v14, 16)
- What should our attitude be? (v15)

James is talking to the rich guys in the church who seemed to think that their well-being and security rested entirely in their own hands. They believed in God, but a God with no active involvement in their lives. Not only had these people no thought for God, they had no thought for others either (v17).

THINK IT OVER

Our plans need to fit in with God's plans for us. We must seek His will for our lives. Think about your major plans for the next month, year and 5 years. How do they reflect your attitude to God and your priorities in life?

PRAY ABOUT IT

Say sorry to God for times you've bad-mouthed others or left God out of your plans. Ask for His help in becoming less judgmental. Ask Him to show you His plans for you.

→ TAKE IT FURTHER

Check out the view on page 113.

24 | Rich pickings

James warned the richer members of the church not to think they were in control of their lives or could ignore others' needs. Talking about money made James angry, and he blasted into greedy rich people in general.

👁 Read James 5 v 1–3

ENGAGE YOUR BRAIN

- 🔘 What will happen to wealth and possessions eventually? (v2–3)
- 🔘 What had they done with their money? (v3)

If God gives us stuff, we should share it with others — especially people who don't have much. James says it's the "last days" — one day Jesus will return to judge those who live for themselves. And to gather believers for a much better life with Him. Don't hoard wealth and possessions as if life on earth is all there is.

👁 Read verses 4–6

Ok, it's unlikely you've failed to pay workmen or murdered innocent victims. Think of examples from your life that match the attitudes in these verses:

v4:

v5:

v6:

It's so easy to be greedy and selfish. James says don't rip people off or take advantage of others. Don't waste money on luxury and self-indulgence. Don't let greed turn you against people who don't deserve it.

GET ON WITH IT

- 🔘 How does your attitude towards life on earth and your possessions need to change?
- 🔘 How can you share stuff you usually keep to yourself?
- 🔘 How will you use your possessions to please God?
- 🔘 Who do you treat badly?
- 🔘 Who do you rip off?
- 🔘 What luxuries in your life are unnecessary and over the top?

PRAY ABOUT IT

Talk to God about anything He's challenged you about today.

→ TAKE IT FURTHER

Aim for Amos on page 113.

25 | Wait for it |

How patient are you? How good are you at waiting for good stuff to happen? James says Christians need to be patient, waiting for Jesus to return. And to be patient with those greedy types from yesterday.

👁 Read James 5 v 7–11

ENGAGE YOUR BRAIN

▶ *How should we live this life? (v7–8)*
▶ *What shouldn't we do? (v9)*
▶ *How is Job a great example?*
▶ *What does his amazing story show us about God? (v11)*

Life here and now isn't all there is. One day, Jesus will return. Christians will go on to something much better. And God will judge those who reject Him. So we shouldn't waste this life judging others and complaining about them. Even those who are selfish and greedy.

Christians are to be patient, keeping living for God, knowing a perfect life with God is on the horizon. That means suffering in this life at times. Though none of us will suffer as much as Job did. But he didn't turn against God, and the Lord rewarded Him greatly and showed His immense love and compassion.

👁 Read verse 12

In Bible times, people would make a promise ("I'll feed your camel every day") with an oath attached ("I swear it by heaven"). It was thought if you didn't add an oath then you didn't have to keep your word. Crazy. This was twisting God's law and it led to loads of lying.

We shouldn't just keep promises if we use the words "I promise". Christians should be truthful all the time, and keep their word. If you say you will do something — make sure you do it!

PRAY ABOUT IT

▶ *Are you grumbling?*
▶ *Are you patient?*
▶ *Is your word reliable?*
▶ *Are you persevering, with eternity and God's judgment in view?*

Talk your answers through with God.

→ TAKE IT FURTHER

Jesus' view can be found on p113.

26 ┆ Survival guide ┆

Life can be tough in this world for Christians. James has told us to be patient and to keep going as we wait for eternity with Jesus. Next, he gives us some more survival tips.

👁 Read James 5 v 13

ENGAGE YOUR BRAIN

▶ *Be honest, what do you do to cope when life is hard?*

▶ *And what do you do to show you're happy in life?*

▶ *How does James say Christians should react in these situations?*

If we're finding life hard, let's pray as a first resort, not last. If we're happy, let's thank God. It's down to Him.

👁 Read verses 14–18

▶ *What's the advice for when a Christian is sick? (v14–15)*

▶ *And what about when we've done wrong? (v15–16)*

▶ *What does Elijah's example remind us about God? (v17–18)*

If someone you know is ill, grab other Christians to pray for them.

Remember, God always answers our prayers, although not always in the way we might expect. It's not always God's plan to instantly heal people.

It's a great idea to regularly get together with other Christians to pray. As well as just hanging out, you can talk about the sin you're struggling with and pray about it (v16).

PRAY ABOUT IT

If you're in trouble, ask God to help you.

If you're happy, praise Him!

If you're ill, ask God to make you better.

If you've done wrong, admit it to God and say sorry.

→ TAKE IT FURTHER

Still surviving? Go to page 113.

27 ┊ Don't just stand there! ┊

You're standing at the train station waiting for the 4.20 to Rochdale. To your horror, you see a doddery old man wandering dangerously close to the edge as a fast train is approaching.

▶ *Do you...*
a) look the other way and hope for the best?
b) assume someone else will save him?
c) run to him and guide him away from the edge?

◉ **Read James 5 v 19–20**

Hannah is a friend from church. She's always said she's a Christian, but recently she's been going off the rails. You're worried she'll choose her non-Christian friends and boyfriend over church, and give up on Christianity.

▶ *Do you...*
a) look the other way and hope for the best?
b) assume someone else will save her?
c) calmly chat with her, trying to point her back to living God's way?
d) pray for her loads?
e) if she won't listen, ask an older Christian to help?

Hopefully you chose c, d and e! Often when we see a friend turning away from God, we're too scared to say anything to them. Or we just gossip about them behind their backs.

Sin shouldn't be a private matter. Christians are to be responsible and accountable to each other. So, each of us must seek to live right and must get involved in helping others.

PRAY ABOUT IT

Is there anyone you're worried will turn away from God? Ask God to bring them back to living His way. And think how you might be able to lovingly point them back in the right direction.

TAKE IT FURTHER

Don't just stand there, do something!

→ **TAKE IT FURTHER**

One last look at James on page 114.

STUFF

Self-harm & eating disorders

Sometimes life hurts. That's what happens in a world that ignores God. The pressure of exams crash in. The taunts of a bully get too much. Someone we care about dies. The person we thought we could trust betrays us. And we're left feeling awful and have to find ways of handling the pain.

WHAT ARE SELF-HARM AND EATING DISORDERS?

We all have different ways of dealing with problems. A few handle life's pain by restricting their food intake (anorexia), eating loads and then throwing up (bulimia), eating excessively (compulsive eating) or hurting themselves by hitting, cutting or overdosing (self-harm). You might know someone who is doing just that. Maybe you're doing it yourself.

HOW DO SELF-HARM AND EATING DISORDERS WORK?

People who do these things aren't crazy. What they're doing makes sense to them. It provides a little:

Control

Sometimes we feel everything is out of control. Some people respond to that by trying to reclaim control.

They may not have power over much but they will dictate what food goes into their body or what happens to their skin.

Punishment

There are days when we feel guilt (about stuff we've done wrong) or false guilt (when we feel things are our fault even when they're not). Some people respond by punishing themselves, maybe through self-harm or depriving themselves of something they need.

Cleansing

If the pressure of negative emotions builds up, we can feel as if we're going to explode. Some people try to release the pressure by trying to get rid of the bad stuff inside by vomiting or putting a hole in their skin.

Relief

When life really hurts, most of us wish we could turn down the pain. Some people respond by numbing themselves with large quantities of food or drugs.

For a while, doing these things makes life feel a little more manageable. But that feeling doesn't last. Bodies get weaker — sometimes dangerously so. Emotions become more negative. And people feel as if God is far away and doesn't care.

IS THERE A BETTER WAY?

The reality is that God isn't far away from Christians who are struggling. He's right alongside us, comforting us. He's busy encouraging us to change (Romans 8 v 28–29). And pointing us to better ways of dealing with the pain of a sinful world. He doesn't want us to grab control of our lives but to trust Jesus, the awesome King of the universe.

Instead of us punishing ourselves, He wants us to accept that Jesus took our punishment when He hung on the cross. Rather than us striving to get the bad stuff out of us, He wants us to know that we are loved beyond measure and made totally clean (1 John 1 v 9). And instead of us squishing our emotions or silently enduring pain, He longs for us to have life — life in all its fullness (John 10 v 10).

He has given us His Spirit to live inside us so we can change. With His help, and the help of wise Christians, people can and do recover from self-harm and eating disorders, and they learn new, better ways of dealing with the pain of this world.

SO WHAT NEXT?

If you are struggling with any of these issues – or know someone who is — why not talk to your parents, youth leader, pastor or doctor? Don't keep it to yourself. They will be able to help you. And ask God to help too. None of us will be completely sorted until Jesus returns, but we can all gradually change to be more like Him ... starting today!

28 | Ezekiel: Know God, know hope

Ezekiel, the story so far: God's people in Judah had rejected Him. God would punish them severely and unstoppably. Ezekiel gives us all the graphic details. And yet he also offers hope for God's people.

👁 Read Ezekiel 16 v 1–14

ENGAGE YOUR BRAIN

- ▶ *How are the people of Jerusalem described? (v4–5)*
- ▶ *What did God do for "baby" Jerusalem? (v6–7)*
- ▶ *What else did He do for His people? (v8)*
- ▶ *How would you describe God's treatment of His people? (v9–13)*

👁 Skim read verses 15–29

- ▶ *How did God's people respond to His love and generosity? (v15, 17, 20, 25–26)*
- ▶ *Did they trust and rely on God or on themselves? (v15)*

👁 Quickly read verses 30–42

- ▶ *How did the people of Jerusalem treat God? (v32)*
- ▶ *How did they treat God's enemies? (v33)*
- ▶ *How would God use these nations to punish His people? (v38–41)*
- ▶ *Would God's anger end? (v42)*

👁 Skim read verses 43–58

- ▶ *How did Judah react to the sin of its neighbours? (v46–48)*

👁 Slowly read verses 59–63

- ▶ *How would God treat His disobedient people? (v59)*
- ▶ *What was the astonishing news? (v60)*
- ▶ *What effect would it have on them? (v62–63)*

God's people were like a rejected baby who God turned into a beauty queen who lacked nothing. Yet they turned against Him and broke their covenant agreement. Rightly, God would punish them. And yet He would replace the broken covenant with an unbreakable one (through Jesus' death).

THINK IT OVER

- ▶ *What's this chapter brought home to you?*

→ TAKE IT FURTHER

The missing chapter is on page 114.

29 | Tall tree tale

God gave Ezekiel another story to tell the people. It involved two powerful eagles and a beautiful tree. It was all about Jerusalem, it's king and what would happen over the next five years and into the future.

👁 Read Ezekiel 17 v 1–21

ENGAGE YOUR BRAIN

- ▶ Who were the first eagle and the tree? (v3, 12)
- ▶ What did the king of Babylon do? (v4–6, 12–14)
- ▶ But what did Zedekiah, King of Judah, do? (v7, 15)
- ▶ What happened to the plant? (v9–10)
- ▶ What would happen to Zedekiah and his army? (v16, 20–21)
- ▶ Why? (v18–19)

Zedekiah and Judah had been conquered by Babylon. They turned to Egypt for help and rebelled against Babylon, so King Nebuchadnezzar destroyed Zedekiah and his army. Judah had also rebelled against God (v19) and there's no escape from God's punishment (v20). But...

👁 Read verses 22–24

- ▶ What would God do with the tree? (v22)
- ▶ What would happen? (v23)

Despite their hideous rebellion, God hadn't finished with His people. A shoot would grow out of this rotten tree and grow into something amazing. God would send Jesus to rescue His people and make them fruitful again.

Ezekiel's message, far from being one of just "doom and gloom", is all about Jesus Christ coming into the world to save sinners. God is in control of history. He's the one in charge of the world, not billionaires or military regimes. And one day, everyone will realise it (v24).

THINK IT OVER

If God's in charge of history and the whole world, how should this affect the way you view:
a) God?
b) what's happening in the world?
c) you place in the world?

→ TAKE IT FURTHER

Fly on over to page 114.

37

30 | Sour grapes

Back in Ezekiel's day, many people believed in the idea of "inherited guilt" — if your father or son (or mother or daughter) sinned, God would punish you for it too. Ezekiel was about to bust that myth completely.

👁 Read Ezekiel 18 v 1–13

ENGAGE YOUR BRAIN

- ◗ *How is "sour grapes" (v2) used differently here to how we use it?*
- ◗ *What was the definition of a righteous man? (v5–9)*
- ◗ *And an evil man? (v10–13)*
- ◗ *What were the different outcomes for these two men? (v9, 13)*

A common phrase in Jerusalem was: *"The fathers eat sour grapes, and the children's teeth are set on edge"*. This meant that if a father did something wrong, his kids would be punished. Ezekiel said that's nonsense. Everyone is responsible for themselves before God. Those who are right with God will live and those who don't will die.

👁 Skim read verses 14–29

- ◗ *Just a reminder, would a son be punished for his dad's sin? (v17)*
- ◗ *Why not? (v19)*
- ◗ *Who will God punish? (v20)*
- ◗ *Can "wicked" people get right with God? (v21–22)*
- ◗ *And can a "good" person turn away from God and face His punishment? (v24)*

👁 Read verses 30–32

- ◗ *What's the message for everyone? (v30–31)*
- ◗ *Why does God tell us these things? (v32)*

The fact is, no one can live a good enough life for God. That's why He sent Jesus to take the punishment we deserve. Only those who trust in Jesus will receive eternal life. The message for everyone is: "Repent! Turn away from your sin. Turn back to God. Trust in Jesus for forgiveness. Receive a new heart and a new spirit."

PRAY ABOUT IT

Read verses 30–32 again and talk through your thoughts with God.

→ TAKE IT FURTHER

Another missing chapter is located on page 114.

31 History mystery

Ezekiel has been deliverying God's messages of punishment to His disobedient people. And a warning to repent. Finally, some of Israel's elders went to Ezekiel. Would he welcome them with open arms?

👁 **Read Ezekiel 20 v 1–29**

ENGAGE YOUR BRAIN

▷ What shock did God have for these leaders? (v2–3)
▷ What did He tell Ezekiel to talk to those leaders about? (v4)
▷ What had God done for them?
v5–7:
v9–12:
v14–20:
▷ How had they responded? (v8, 13, 16, 21)
▷ What did God do eventually? (v22–26)

This is the pattern of the Old Testament. God did awesome things for His people. They rejected Him and sinned horrifically. Incredibly, God kept His promises to His people and continued to rescue them. He did this so that His reputation ("name") was honoured (v9).

👁 **Read verses 30–44**

▷ What did these exiles' actions show about their attitude to God? (v30–32)
▷ What was God's response? (v33–35)
▷ What would He achieve? (v38–39)
▷ What was the future for those who stayed faithful to God? (v40–41)
▷ How would this affect God's people? (v42–44)

God's people would be brought out of Babylon... to face His punishment (v35). And yet, a handful who did still trust God would have a future as God's true people.

PRAY ABOUT IT

Thank God that even in His judgment and punishment, He is completely fair. Thank Him that He offers rescue to those who trust Him. Pray that you'll be able to get His message across to those who need to turn back to God.

→ **TAKE IT FURTHER**
Fiery stuff on page 115.

32 ¦ Sinful sisters

We're going to try something different today. Shortly, we'll ask you to read all of chapter 23. Just like that. In one go. Take your time.

It's another message of judgment from God, through Ezekiel, to God's people (don't groan!). It's in the form of a story. There are two characters. Sisters, called Oholah and Oholibah. Strange names.

The first represents Samaria, Israel's capital. The other represents Jerusalem, capital of Judah. So the story's another mini-history. From God's viewpoint.

And it's graphic. At times rude. Disgusting. Tasteless. Cheap. Sordid. But that's how God's people had behaved and how they treated Him.

It works like this:
v1–10: about Oholah (Samaria)
v11–21: about Oholibah (Jerusalem)
v22–35: Oholibah's fate
v36–49: judgment on both.

👁 Read Ezekiel 23

Jot down any thoughts or questions you have as you read.

ENGAGE YOUR BRAIN

▶ *How had God's people repeatedly treated Him?*

▶ *Why is that behaviour described as prostitution?*

▶ *What would God's judgment involve?*

▶ *What warning does this chapter give you?*

PRAY ABOUT IT

Say sorry to God for times you've treated Him like this. Ask for His help in becoming more and more faithful to Him.

TAKE IT FURTHER

Two more missing chapters on p115.

33 Devastating news

The time has come. God's words of judgment from chapter 12 onwards now start to happen. "No God, no hope" will be clearly, horribly, personally demonstrated.

⊚ Read Ezekiel 24 v 1–14

ENGAGE YOUR BRAIN

ⅅ *It's January 588BC — why is that date significant? (v2)*

ⅅ *What happened in the cooking pot story? (v3–5)*

ⅅ *What was God teaching about Jerusalem? (v13–14)*

The heat's on. Jerusalem won't be left a ghost town, but will be an inferno of destruction. Cooked till it roasts. All because of God's punishment of His people's wrongdoing.

⊚ Read verses 15–27

ⅅ *What devastating tthing did God do to Ezekiel? (v16–18)*

ⅅ *What was God teaching His people? (v20–24)*

ⅅ *What was Ezekiel to look out for later? (v25–27)*

Shocking. Ezekiel had to endure the death of his own wife in order to teach the exiles about God's judgment on their beloved Jerusalem. And there was no room for mourning. God's punishment would leave people numb and speechless.

Chapters 1–24 have spelled out God's message of judgment on His people. There was no hope for them... until God had punished them. But there will be hope. Honestly. Though next (chapters 25–32), we'll see God punishing Israel's evil enemies.

PRAY ABOUT IT

Thank God for His justice even though we don't always understand it. Pray for people you know who are facing His judgment if they carry on rejecting Him.

→ TAKE IT FURTHER

Shocked and angry about the death of Ezekiel's wife? Read more on p115.

34 | Condemn nations

So the siege of Jerusalem began (24 v 2). But before we're told of the city's destruction (in chapter 33), Ezekiel preached about God's attitude to other nations. Here's four for starters:

👁 Read Ezekiel 25 v 1–11

ENGAGE YOUR BRAIN

- ▷ *What had Amman done? (v6)*
- ▷ *What were the consequences? (v4, 7)*
- ▷ *What would the Ammonites realise? (v5)*
- ▷ *What had Moab done? (v8)*
- ▷ *What were the consequences? (v9–10)*
- ▷ *What would the Moabites realise? (v11)*

👁 Read verses 12–17

- ▷ *What had Edom done? (v12)*
- ▷ *What were the consequences? (v13)*
- ▷ *What had Philistia done? (v15)*
- ▷ *What were the consequences? (v16–17)*
- ▷ *What would the Edomites and Philistines know? (v14, 17)*

These four nations mocked God and His people. They delighted when Judah failed. They took revenge on God's people. But they would have to accept that Judah's God was Lord of all, and face the consequences.

God rules the world. The punishment He brought in Jerusalem didn't stop there. The world that defied Him would be overthrown too. They'd be brought to know who He really is.

THINK IT OVER

- ▷ *Do you realise who God is and how seriously He views sin?*
- ▷ *How do you need to take God more seriously?*

PRAY ABOUT IT

Thank God that He rightly and fairly punishes His enemies and those who attack and persecute His people. Pray that you'll take sin — and take God — more seriously.

TAKE IT FURTHER

Extra stuff on page 115.

35 | Tyre punctured

While Jerusalem is under siege, Ezekiel speaks again of God acting against other nations in power and justice. To make them see who He is. Next up? Tyre, a prosperous port 100 miles northwest of Jerusalem.

◉ Read Ezekiel 26 v 1–21

ENGAGE YOUR BRAIN

▷ *What was Tyre's crime? (v2)*

▷ *What were the consequences?*
v3–6:
v7–14:
v19–21:

Tyre, the island fortress. The money-spinning mega city. Flattened to a rock (v4). It seemed unthinkable. But mess with God and that's what you get. No wonder Tyre's end would spread utter terror (v16–18).

◉ Read Ezekiel 28 v 1–10

▷ *What had the king of Tyre done? (v2–5)*

▷ *So what would happen? (v6–10)*

◉ Read Ezekiel 28 v 20–26

▷ *What would God's punishment of Sidon achieve? (v22–23)*

▷ *What was the amazing news for God's people? (v24–26)*

Bad news for God's enemies — they would pay a huge price for their rebellion. Great news for God's people — He would gather them and take them home. Before that, He would act in terrifying judgment. Only then would His people, and the nations, accept His fearsomely fair wordwide rule.

PRAY ABOUT IT
When you talk to God, remember how awesome and powerful He is. Do you ever make God too small or forget how immense and all-conquering He is? We are *His* possession, not the other way round. Give God the correct respect as you talk to Him today.

→ TAKE IT FURTHER
There's a sad song on page 116.

36 | The end for Egypt

Next enemy in the line of fire is Egypt. And rightly so: Egypt had persecuted God's people massively over the centuries. And its destruction would teach God's people a vital lesson too.

👁 Read Ezekiel 29 v 1–16

ENGAGE YOUR BRAIN

▶ *What was Pharaoh's attitude? (v3)*

▶ *So how would God treat Pharaoh and his people? (v4–5)*

▶ *How had Egypt treated God's people? (v6–7)*

▶ *How would God punish Egypt? (v8–12)*

▶ *What was the future for Egypt the bully? (v13–15)*

▶ *What would this teach God's people? (v16)*

The Egyptians had persecuted God's people for centuries, enslaving them and massacring them. Yet the Israelites had still turned to Egypt for help, instead of crying out to the Lord! God's punishment of Egypt would show His people who they should put their trust in.

👁 Read verses 17–21

▶ *Who would carry out God's punishment on Egypt? (v19)*

Ezekiel made this announcement 17 years after the previous one. Babylon conquered Egypt just 3 years later. As always, what God promised, happened. Verse 21 is saying that God would restore His people. He controls the whole world, even superpowers like Babylon and Egypt. He's the one people should trust in and turn to. In God alone is hope.

THINK IT OVER

▶ *Where do you turn to for help before turning to God?*

▶ *In what areas of life do you need to trust God more?*

PRAY ABOUT IT

Praise God that He's in complete control. Talk to Him about times when you rely on yourself and other people, not Him. Pray that you'll trust Him more.

TAKE IT FURTHER

Hunt down chapter 30 on page 116.

37 | No rest for the wicked

Ezekiel's still telling us what God would do to Pharaoh and his evil hordes. Ezekiel uses imaginative language to describe Egypt's fate, mentioning tall trees, sea monsters and lots of blood.

👁 Read Ezekiel 31 v 1–9

ENGAGE YOUR BRAIN

- ▶ *Egypt was like Assyria (an earlier empire). How? (v2–3)*
- ▶ *What was this tree like? (v4–9)*

👁 Skim read verses 10–18

- ▶ *What was the problem? (v10)*
- ▶ *So what did God do? (v11)*
- ▶ *What would happen to Egypt? (v12–18)*

Pharaoh thought he was brilliant and unstoppable like a tall, beautiful tree. Like Assyria before, God would chop Egypt down to size. No nations, however mighty, are a match for God.

👁 Skim read Ezekiel 32 v 1–16

- ▶ *How is Pharaoh described? (v2)*
- ▶ *What would God do with this terrifying sea monster? (v3–6)*
- ▶ *What effect would Egypt's destruction have on the world? (v7–10)*

👁 Read verses 17–32

- ▶ *How would you describe this picture of hell?*
- ▶ *What's the fate of God's enemies?*

However successful "wicked" people seem, there's only one outcome for God's enemies — hell. It's a deliberately horrible picture. We should be shocked that people around us are heading to hell. And we must do something about it.

SHARE IT

- ▶ *Who do you avoid talking to about Christian stuff?*
- ▶ *Who will you offer the hope of Jesus to this week?*

PRAY ABOUT IT

Let today's vision of hell shock you into praying for as many non-Christians as you can think of.

Well done for surving Ezekiel part 2. Part 3 will be more hope-filled!

NO TAKE IT FURTHER TODAY

REAL LIVES

Anand's story

Anand was brought up in a Hindu family in the UK and later got into the drug scene. Here's his story in his own words.

What was your view about Jesus when you were growing up?

I was always drawn to Jesus as a child even though I was from a Hindu background and never visited a church. There was something wonderful and approachable about Jesus compared to the lofty Hindu gods. They were only images on a wall, nothing like as tangible as Jesus. I particularly remember hearing about how Jesus allowed the little children into His presence when others drove them away. In fact, just about anything I heard He said was so clear and right, His appeal was magnetic!

How did you get to hear about Jesus when you were brought up as a Hindu?

I heard about Jesus and was exposed to His teaching in all kinds of different ways — either through television programmes, through parables of Jesus the headmaster used to tell us in assembly or even through films like Jesus of Nazareth or Jesus Christ Superstar! That might make us Christians cringe because their teaching is sometimes incorrect but they were powerful to non-Christians like me!

What made you decide to follow Jesus?

I was brought up in an area that was predominantly Asian, so I had very little contact with any Christians growing up. However I met Marcus, who was a Christian, when we were both 17. He was on fire for God, praying and seeking to win souls. God eventually led him to speak to me at a time when the Lord was already beginning to open my heart to his

word. Taking time to read about Jesus in the Gospels was the best thing as it led me to become a Christian.

How did your family react?

It was hard for me to tell my dad, initially, as I was worried about how he would react. However, he just thought it was another one of my phases and that I'd grow out of it. But when my brother became a Christian, that's when he thought "this is serious" and tried to dissuade us from being Christians.

My brother was the total opposite of me. He was the perfect son, with top grades at school and uni, whereas I was into the drug culture. My dad complained that we were reading the Bible all the time, and he even complained to our church pastor that we weren't spending enough time studying.

Our pastor pointed out that this wasn't true as he was always encouraging us to study well and bring glory to God in our studies. This was a real turning point for my dad. He started understanding that church people were after our best interests rather than trying to take them away. He slowly started warming up and accepting that we were now Christians. Although dad passed away a number of years ago, my mother amazingly became a Christian two years ago.

What difference does knowing Jesus make to your life now?

I have now been a Christian for 20 years — it's made all the difference and continues to do so because I depend on Him for everything. The light of Christ's truth contained in the Bible exposes me at the core and causes me to repent and turn to Him. Like the prodigal son, I came to my senses and went back to the Father. How people in this world go on without Jesus I'll never know!

Matthew

Are you ready?

How do you tend to get ready? Are you a planning-ahead, well-prepared kind of person? Or do you usually leave things till the last minute and hope for the best?

As we dive back into Matthew's Gospel, picking up the story in chapter 23, we meet a King who is ready — ready to die. Jesus, the all-powerful, eternally-ruling "Son of Man", is in Jerusalem, surrounded by His followers and His opponents.

And He knows that *"the Son of Man will be handed over to be crucified"* (26 v 2). He knows that it's time for all the Old Testament prophecies about Him to be fulfilled. He knows that it's time to pour out His blood so that His followers can be forgiven (v28). Jesus knows that the moment He was born for, that His life has been preparing for, is about to come — His death. The King is ready to die.

But in His final teachings, during His arrest, even as He hangs on the cross, we'll see Him getting His followers ready, too. Ready to live. Jesus knows

His death will not be the end.

He points us to the day *"when the Son of Man comes in his glory, and all the angels with him, [and] he will sit on his throne in heavenly glory"* (25 v 31). He warns people to be ready for His return, ready to welcome Him and enjoy eternal life with Him. And He tells us how to live in a way which shows we're ready for the day when the King comes again.

So as we spend time with Jesus in His final few days before death… as we follow Him through His arrest, on to His cross, into His tomb and beyond… as we watch His enemies plot against Him, His friends fail to back Him, and even His Father God completely desert Him… we'll see a King who loves His people so much He's ready to die for them.

And we'll see Him call us to be ready to live. Get ready to get ready!

38 | Rotten religion

One of the shocks of the Gospels is that Jesus and religion just don't get on. In fact, Jesus is about to give the religious leaders of His day both barrels...

👁 Read Matthew 23 v 1–7

The "teachers of the law and the Pharisees" led Israel's religious life (v2). They were the bishops and pastors of their day. Surely they had religion sorted...

ENGAGE YOUR BRAIN

▶ *But how does Jesus criticise them? (end of v3, end of v5)*

▶ *What do they love most? (v6–7)*

THINK ABOUT IT

These guys do a lot of very religious stuff. But it's rotten. Imagine this kind of person, with those kind of aims, was part of your church. What would they do, and be like?

PRAY ABOUT IT

Lord Jesus, help me never to make my religion about me. Help me never to use my Christianity to try to look good in front of other people. Amen.

👁 Read verses 8–12

These leaders loved to have impressive-sounding titles (v7). Today, they'd want to be addressed as "The Right Very Especially Reverend Dr So-and-So".

▶ *What does Jesus say His true followers should do? (v8–10)*

▶ *What should their motivation be? (v11)*

Spot the difference? These religious leaders want others to look up to them; Jesus' followers are to get on their hands and knees to serve others. That's the point in v12. Christians don't need to big themselves up. God will do it for them.

PRAY ABOUT IT

Lord, help me to serve your people as I follow you, and rely on you to give me the glory of eternal life.

→ TAKE IT FURTHER

Spoil yourself rotten on page 116.

39 Pulling no punches

Jesus' words here are as hardcore as you can get. "Woe" is a way of saying "God's condemnation and anger". With that in mind...

👁 Read Matthew 23 v 13-22

ENGAGE YOUR BRAIN

▷ *How many times does Jesus promise "woe" here, and who to?*

▷ *What reasons does He give?*
v13:
v15:
v16–22:

These men are very, very religious. They take it very seriously.

▷ *What are they willing to do in order to convert someone to their way of thinking? (v15)*

▷ *That's evangelism — great! Isn't it? (end of v15)*

THINK ABOUT IT
Here's the sting. It's possible to be religious, hardworking, committed and successful — and at the same time be condemning yourself, and leading others towards hell (v15). It doesn't matter if you really believe

something. What matters is believing something real. The road to hell can be a very religious one.

▷ *Re-read v10. What is the right way to be religious?*

GET ON WITH IT
In one way, we should be the opposite of the Pharisees.
▷ *How should we act differently from the Pharisees? (v13)*

In another way, we can learn from the Pharisees.
▷ *How far were they willing to go to get just one person to believe what they did? (v15)*

▷ *How does this challenge you?*

THE BOTTOM LINE
You can be very religious and go to hell: make sure you're following Christ into His kingdom.

→ TAKE IT FURTHER
Grab some more on page 116.

40 Good looks

Are you good-looking? Jesus says you won't find the answer in a mirror.

◉ Read Matthew 23 v 23–28

ENGAGE YOUR BRAIN
▷ *What do the leaders do? What don't they do? (v23–24)*

It's not only giving 1/10th they are hot on: it's also cleaning anything they eat food from (v25). So Jesus uses a cup and dish as a picture of the religious leaders themselves.

▷ *What's the problem? (v25)*

▷ *What should they be focusing on? (v26)?*

▷ *How does Jesus' image in v27–28 repeat the point He's making?*

THINK ABOUT IT
▷ *If you were looking at a Pharisee, how good-looking, in religious terms, would they seem?*

▷ *But Jesus doesn't care about the outside. What does He say really matters?*

▷ *How would it be possible for you to be good-looking on the outside, and ugly on the inside?*

GET ON WITH IT
Look at your heart. Really look hard! Have you asked Jesus to be in charge of it? Have you asked Jesus to take away all the wrong in it? Or are you just looking good at church, on the outside, to hide the fact that there are all kinds of "wickedness" in your heart which you really enjoy and don't want to get rid of?

PRAY ABOUT IT
Ask God to let you see the state of your heart. Ask Him to help you never to cover up an ugly inside, but instead to ask Jesus to deal with it.

THE BOTTOM LINE
The world cares about our outside: Jesus cares about our heart.

→ TAKE IT FURTHER
Hey good looking, look at page 117.

41 | Jesus' wings

The "woes" continue. Is there any way these guys can escape hell? Yes! But will they take it?

👁 **Read Matthew 24 v 29–36**

Israel had a long history of killing God's messengers instead of listening to them (v31). But that was a long time ago — in Jesus' day, the leaders said they would never make that mistake (v30).

But now God's Son had come. And He would send "prophets and wise men and teachers" to Israel, to call God's ancient people to truly know and serve God.

ENGAGE YOUR BRAIN

▶ *How would these religious leaders treat them? (v34)*

PRAY ABOUT IT

It's easy to think how stupid these men were for shutting up Jesus' messengers instead of listening to them. But isn't that exactly what we do whenever we don't bother to read or remember or obey their words in the Bible?

Speak to God now. Admit to Him the times this week you've ignored people He's spoken through in the Bible.

👁 **Read verses 37–39**

The Jews of Jerusalem deserve "being condemned to hell" (v33).

▶ *But what does Jesus want to do? (v37)*

A hen does this to protect her children from harm. When God's judgment on those who have rejected Him is unleashed, there will only be one safe place in the universe: under Jesus' wings. Tragically, these guys didn't want that (v37).

PRAY ABOUT IT

Tell God, for the first or thousandth time, that you're putting yourself under Jesus' protection, to avoid the judgment you deserve and enjoy the eternal life He gives.

→ **TAKE IT FURTHER**

Fly over to page 117.

42 The end of the world

**Warning: Matthew 24 is hard.
But it's well worth the effort!**

👁 Read Matthew 24 v 1–3

ENGAGE YOUR BRAIN
▶ What does Jesus predict? (v1–2)

▶ What two questions do His followers ask Him? (v3)

Verse 3 is the key to the whole chapter. Jesus is talking about two events at the same time. One is the destruction of the temple, and the whole of Jerusalem. This was Jesus' judgment on Israel for rejecting Him, and happened in AD70. The other is the destruction of the entire world at "the end of the age". This will be His judgment on the whole of humanity, and hasn't happened yet!

What happened to Israel in AD70 was a catastrophe. But it was just a picture of God's final judgment. And as Jesus told His followers how to live waiting for His judgment of Israel, He was also telling Christians in 2012 how to live awaiting His final judgment.

👁 Read verses 4–14
▶ What will happen before Jesus returns? (v4–9)

▶ What will happen within the Christian community? (v10–12)

▶ So what must we do? (v13–14)

For people who do that, there will be rescue from judgment (v13). For those who keep going with Jesus, "the end" will in fact be a beginning, of perfect life in a perfect world.

GET ON WITH IT
▶ How do Jesus' words here help you keep going when it's hard to be a Christian?

THE BOTTOM LINE
"He who stands firm to the end will be saved."

→ TAKE IT FURTHER
Make sure you end up on page 117.

43 Where's the world heading?

Environmental disaster? Nuclear destruction? Robots taking over? Aliens landing? Nope…

👁 Read Matthew 24 v 15–28

ENGAGE YOUR BRAIN

Again, Jesus is mixing details that are only about the fall of Jerusalem (v15–16, 20) with details about the end of the world (v21).

▷ *What do His followers need to be particularly careful about? (v23–26)*
▷ *What will these fakes be able to do? (v24)*

If we saw someone who could do these things, we'd be very impressed! And we'd probably listen to what they had to say — after all, surely someone who can do these amazing feats must be from God?! But Jesus says: "No!" Don't be influenced by someone just because they can do miracles and impressive stuff.

▷ *Flick your eyes down to v35. What counts much more than miracles?*

GET ON WITH IT

Don't be impressed by powerful teachers, witty speakers, impressive leaders. Be impressed by those who point you to Jesus' eternal words. We don't need to worry that we might miss Jesus' return. It will be totally obvious to absolutely everyone (v27).

👁 Read verses 29–35

▷ *What will happen to the creation? (v29)*
▷ *And to Jesus? (v30)*
▷ *And to "the nations", who don't know Jesus? (v30)*
▷ *And to Christians ("the elect")? (v31)*

THINK ABOUT IT

▷ *How does all this motivate you to keep living for Jesus today?*

THE BOTTOM LINE

When Jesus returns, the world will fall, but His people will be with Him.

→ TAKE IT FURTHER

Head on over to page 117.

44 | And then BANG!

Today is pretty much like yesterday. Tomorrow will probably be the same. The world turns, life continues, nothing much changes... AND THEN BANG!

👁 Read Matthew 5 v 36–44

ENGAGE YOUR BRAIN
▶ *When will Jesus return? (v36)*

Jesus compares the day He comes to the days of Noah (v37).

▶ *What were people doing? (v38)*

▶ *AND THEN BANG! What happened? (v39)*

▶ *So what is Jesus saying about His return? (v40-41)*

The world's destined for destruction (v29). But Jesus will gather His people so they avoid that destruction (v31). One day, everyone will be going about their everyday business, just like the day before, AND THEN BANG. And you don't want to be left behind.

▶ *What's the right response? (v42)*

👁 Read verses 45–51
Jesus is explaining how we know

whether we're ready for Him to return to His world. All of us have been given ways to help His people, "the servants" (v45).

▶ *What does Jesus, "the master", want to find us doing when He returns? (v46)*

▶ *What will He then do? (v47)*

Exciting stuff! But if, instead, we live for ourselves, abusing our privileges (v48-49), then we're showing we don't really think Jesus will return (v50). We're not ready. We'll face an eternity outside His kingdom (v51).

THINK ABOUT IT
▶ *Are you ready to welcome Him as your Lord and Saviour if it happens today?*

▶ *How will you serve His people while you wait?*

→ TAKE IT FURTHER
More banging on, on page 118.

45

Don't be f-oil-ish

The question keeps coming: are you ready?

👁 Read Matthew 25 v 1–13

ENGAGE YOUR BRAIN

▶ *What's Jesus' point, again? (v13)*

But He's wanting to give a particular warning by telling this parable. The "virgins" (or bridesmaids) have lamps so they can meet the bridegroom, as was traditional.

▶ *What's the only difference between the two kinds of bridesmaids? (v3–4)*

The bridegroom's taking ages to get to the wedding reception, and they all snooze off… (v5). And then suddenly, unexpectedly, he's there (v6)!

▶ *What problem do some of the bridesmaids have? (v8)*

▶ *What do they do?*

▶ *How do the wiser bridesmaids respond? (v9)*

▶ *Where do the bridesmaids who were ready end up?*

▶ *What about those who weren't ready? (v10–13)*

THINK ABOUT IT

The foolish bridesmaids thought they could rely on those around them. But the wiser bridesmaids only had enough oil for themselves. The foolish ones discovered they couldn't rely on anyone else. And they missed out. For virgins/bridesmaids, read "people". For oil, read "faith in Jesus".

▶ *What point is Jesus making?*

GET ON WITH IT

Check you've got real, personal faith in Jesus. When He returns, it won't be enough to say: "My parents know you, Jesus" or "I go to a church which loves you, Jesus" or "When I was younger I followed you, Jesus".

→ TAKE IT FURTHER

Oil for one, one for oil! Page 118.

46 | No time to relax

How do we wait for Jesus' certain return?
Put our feet up and relax till He comes?
Not exactly…

👁 **Read Matthew 25 v 14–30**

ENGAGE YOUR BRAIN

This famous parable is often misunderstood. It's not about making the most of your talents. A master's going on a journey (v14)…

▷ *What does he give his servants? (v15)*

▷ *What do the servants do? (v16–18)*

▷ *When the master returns, how does he respond to: the first servant? (v21) the second? (v23) the third? (v26–30)*

The master expected his servants to use what he'd given them — not just to wait.

THINK ABOUT IT

Jesus is the "master". People who call themselves Christians are the "servants". The crucial thing is to realise that "talents of money" (v15) represent all the circumstances and abilities Jesus has given us.

▷ *Do all Christians have the same circumstances and abilities?*

▷ *How does Jesus want us to use our "talents"?*

GET ON WITH IT

▷ *Have you ever thought: "If I had the ability, or life, or time, that he/she has got, then I'd serve God—but as it is, I can't?"*

▷ *What does this parable have to say about that attitude?*

▷ *Are there any abilities you have that you use for yourself, but never for Jesus?*

▷ *How will you change?*

→ **TAKE IT FURTHER**

Don't relax yet; go to page 118.

47  Be sheepish

As He continues to talk about His return, Jesus takes us into the farmyard.

👁 Read Mattthew 25 v 31–46

ENGAGE YOUR BRAIN

We're fast-forwarding to the end of time, "when the Son of Man comes in his glory" (v31). Can you imagine what a sight that will be? No?! Me neither — it'll be more awe-inspiring than anything we've ever seen.

▷ What will happen to the nations of the world? (v32–33)

▷ Where will the two groups, "sheep" and "goats", end up? (v34, 41)

▷ What makes someone a sheep? (v34–40)

▷ What makes someone a goat? (v42–44)

THINK ABOUT IT

As we've seen (24 v 45–51), how we treat Jesus' people in public shows how we're treating Jesus in our hearts. If someone knows Jesus is their King, they will treat His subjects well.

And if you are a subject of King Jesus, how wonderful to see how much He loves you. You're so close to Him that He sees something kind done for you as being done for Him; if something nasty is done to you, He sees it as nastiness towards Him. And one day, He'll give you everything that's His (v34). That's how much He cares about you!

▷ How should this parable shape your view of your identity?

▷ And your church family?

▷ And your friends who don't know Jesus as King?

PRAY ABOUT IT

Thank Jesus for His love and for your inheritance. Ask Him to give you chances to feed His sheep, and warn the goats.

THE BOTTOM LINE

You come up with it today!

⇨ TAKE IT FURTHER

Follow the sheep to page 118.

48 Beauty in the darkness

Jesus is now just two days from His death. It's going to be an ugly 48 hours: but here we catch a glimpse of beauty.

Read Matthew 26 v 6–13

ENGAGE YOUR BRAIN

- *How is the perfume described? (v7, 9)*

- *Can you understand why the disciples react as they do? (v8–9)*

- *How does Jesus describe what she's done? (v10)*

THINK ABOUT IT

When we give up all we are and all we own for Jesus, as this woman did, the world around us says: "What a waste!" But Jesus Himself says it's "a beautiful thing". And as we honour Jesus, He uses our contribution. We become part of the gospel story, the story of Jesus' death and resurrection and mission throughout the world (v12–13).

GET ON WITH IT

- *In what ways are you living in a way Jesus would say is "beautiful"?*

- *Are there any areas of life you're holding back from Jesus, because they're too precious to you?*

- *Will you let Him have them now?*

Read verses 1–5 and 14–16

- *What is going on while the woman pours her perfume on Jesus?*

Surrounding that woman's actions, we see plotting and betrayal. This world rejects Jesus. But we don't have to. Be like the woman, not like Judas!

PRAY ABOUT IT

Lord Jesus, Thank you that when I do what I can for you, you notice it, you use it, and you say it's beautiful. In a world which rejects you, help me to give everything I am and have in your service today. Amen.

→ TAKE IT FURTHER

Uncover the plot on page 118.

49 | Passover picture

What's the Communion service all about?
What are you meant to think about?
Jesus tells us at the first ever Lord's Supper.

👁 Read Matthew 26 v 17–19

ENGAGE YOUR BRAIN

Matthew tells us it was "the Passover" three times. Passover was the festival where God's people remembered how God had rescued them from slavery in Egypt and brought them into His promised land. He'd told each family He would kill each firstborn son in Egypt — but that they could kill a lamb instead, and not face the same punishment.

👁 Read verses 20–30

As Jesus eats the Passover with His friends, He uses the bread as a picture.

▷ *Of what? (v26)*
▷ *What is the wine a picture of? (v27–28)*
▷ *Jesus is talking about His death. What will the pouring out of His blood achieve? (v28)*
▷ *Jesus is looking forward to something else (v29). What?*

Till this meal, the Passover had been about remembering the rescue from Egypt through a lamb's blood, and how God brought them into the promised land. Jesus is saying that from now on the Passover meal (which we tend to call "Communion") should be about looking at two different events.

▷ *What are they? (v28, 29)*

THINK ABOUT IT

▷ *How do you think the disciples felt as they thought about His death and His kingdom?*
▷ *How does this passage help us know what we should think, and how we should feel, when we share the Communion meal?*

THE BOTTOM LINE

At Communion, we look back to Jesus' death, and forward to being in His kingdom. Take it seriously!

→ TAKE IT FURTHER

Feast some more on page 118.

50 | Scattered

The shepherd says to his flock: ewe are going to be feeling sheep-ish...

👁 Read Matthew 26 v 30—35

ENGAGE YOUR BRAIN

▷ *What does Jesus predict? (v31)*

▷ *Why?*

▷ *How does Peter respond to being told he'll abandon Jesus? (v33, 35)*

Even though Jesus tells Peter he won't stand up for Him, Peter's insistent. He's confident. He's up for it. He won't let Jesus down! But Jesus knows Peter better than Peter knows Peter: he will let Jesus down.

It sounds pretty depressing. That night, God's going to strike Jesus, the shepherd, and the Christian community will be scattered. It sounds like the end of the story.

▷ *Why isn't it? (v32)*

There isn't just hope for Jesus beyond being struck down by God; there's hope for His people too, beyond them deserting Him. They will be together again.

THINK ABOUT IT

It's easy to think Jesus is quite lucky to have us. That He should be pleased we're on His team. That we can do loads to help Him. But this passage reminds us that Jesus' sheep scatter. Left to ourselves, we'll run away from following Jesus. So what matters is not how we serve Jesus, but how He serves us: not how we live as Christians, but how Christ lived and died and rose again for us.

PRAY ABOUT IT

Thank Jesus that He allowed Himself to be struck for you; and that because He rose again, you'll see Him one day. Admit the ways in which you "fall away". Acknowledge that, left to yourself, you can't live for Jesus. Ask for His help now.

→ TAKE IT FURTHER
A little bit more is on page 119.

What is church?

In *Essential*, we take time out to explore key truths about God, the Bible and Christianity. This issue we look at church. How do you use the word "church"? To describe the building you go to each Sunday? The denomination you belong to? Or the people you sit alongside as you learn about Jesus?

The Bible uses the word "church" in three different ways. It is:

1. GOD'S ETERNAL COMMUNITY

The church is all of Jesus' followers throughout time. The apostle Peter is as much part of God's eternal community as we are. So are people like Abraham who looked forward to Jesus in faith (Genesis 15 v 6). Whenever Christians today meet together, we are surrounded by an invisible "cloud of witnesses" (believers who have died and gone to be with Jesus). They are worshipping with us as part of the church (Hebrews 12 v 1).

2. GOD'S GLOBAL COMMUNITY

The Bible also uses the word "church" to represent all Christians who are living on earth right now. Luke describes the Christians of Judea, Galilee and Samaria as being a church (Acts 9 v 31). There were too many of them — and they lived too far away from each other — to actually meet. But Luke still sees them as being one church because they are all part of Jesus' community on earth.

3. GOD'S LOCAL COMMUNITY

Scripture uses the word "church" to describe smaller gatherings of believers in one area. So the Bible refers to the church in Corinth (2 Corinthians 1 v 1) just as we might talk about our local church.

Whether the word "church" is being used to describe something eternal, global or local, it's always used to describe a group of people who have their focus on Jesus. It's never about buildings or organisations. A church is only a church if Jesus is right at the centre of the community. That's because the church is:

A — FOUNDED & BUILT ON JESUS

It is only because of Jesus' death and resurrection that there can be a church. Without His work on the cross, the church couldn't exist because we would be too unclean to have any kind of relationship with God. Jesus is the foundation of the church (Ephesians 2 v 19–20). People only come into the church when Jesus invites them. Jesus builds the church (Matthew 16 v 18) by calling people to become part of it.

B – SERVING JESUS

The church exists to serve Jesus (1 Corinthians 12 v 12–27), who is its head (Ephesians 1 v 22–23). God's community-members spend their time telling others about Jesus (Matthew 28 v 19–20), encouraging each other to grow in their faith (Colossians 1 v 28), praising Jesus (Colossians 3 v 16) and worshipping Him with every part of their lives. (More about exactly what the church does next issue.)

C – JESUS' FAMILY

Jesus' Spirit lives inside each person in the church (Ephesians 2 v 19–22). So each member of the church is "one" in Jesus. We all share the same Father too — God (Ephesians 3 v 14–15). That means the church is basically God's family and it is definitely the best family there is (1 Timothy 5 v 1–2)!

If you think church is boring, you need to remember it was founded and built on Jesus. The church exists because Jesus died for us. And it's a family — an amazing family that includes every believer who ever existed! The question is: how will you get more involved with your Christian family?

63

51 Ezekiel: Know God, know hope

Ezekiel part 3. Yes, there's more violence, judgment and gloom. But this time, hope really starts to shine through for God's people. Yes, really. We promise. But first, Jerusalem finally falls.

👁 Read Ezekiel 33 v 1–11

ENGAGE YOUR BRAIN

- ▶ What's Ezekiel's job? (v7–9)
- ▶ What happened if people ignored his warnings? (v4)
- ▶ Why were God's people being punished? (v10)
- ▶ Does God enjoy punishing people? (v11)
- ▶ What does He want His people to do? (v11)

👁 Read verses 21–33

- ▶ What was the news from Jerusalem? (v21)
- ▶ What stupid hope were the survivors clinging on to? (v24)
- ▶ Why would their wishes not come true? (v25–29)
- ▶ How did the exiles respond to Ezekiel's warnings? (v30–32)
- ▶ What would they eventually realise? (v33)

After 7 years of Ezekiel's warnings, the chilling newsflash came. Yet the survivors in Jerusalem and the exiles in Babylon still didn't get it. They expected God to protect and reward them yet they wouldn't turn from their sinful ways. There's no hope in blind optimism (v24). And there's no hope if you treat God's spokesmen as just entertainment (v32).

GET ON WITH IT

- ▶ Are you ever guilty of blind optimism while still disobeying God?
- ▶ How have you made the mistake of v31?
- ▶ What warnings do you need to react to?
- ▶ What teaching do you need to act on?

THE BOTTOM LINE
"Turn! Turn from your evil ways!"

→ TAKE IT FURTHER
Turn! Turn to page 119.

52 The bad shepherds

Now that Jerusalem has been conquered, Ezekiel can deliver God's message of hope. From destruction... to restoration. But that didn't mean Ezekiel's message suddenly got cuddly and soothing. Think again.

👁 Read Ezekiel 34 v 1–10

ENGAGE YOUR BRAIN

▶ *What does God call Israel's rulers? (v2)*

▶ *How had they acted? (v2–4)*

▶ *So what happened to God's people (the sheep)? (v5–6)*

▶ *What would God do? (v10)*

God's people were like sheep who needed protecting and to be led in the right direction. But Israel's rulers mostly cared only for themselves and treated the people badly. This led to God's people not living God's way and desperately needing a good shepherd.

👁 Read verses 11–16

▶ *What "I will" promises does God make?*

-
-
-
-

-
-
-
-

Amazing. God Himself would rescue His sheepish people. Only He could do it. Notice the love and patience in this incredible section. God would search out His disobedient people, look after them and bring them into their own, safe land. That's more than they could ever hope for. We'll read more about this perfect shepherd tomorrow.

PRAY ABOUT IT

Think of times when God has looked after you. Think of how He's rescued you. Spend time talking to God, showing your gratitude.

THE BOTTOM LINE

The Sovereign Lord says: I myself will search for my sheep and look after them.

➔ TAKE IT FURTHER

Sheepishly turn to page 119.

53 | The Good Shepherd

Israel's leaders had been like bad shepherds, mistreating God's flock. So God was going to sort out the situation Himself.

👁 Read Ezekiel 34 v 17–24

ENGAGE YOUR BRAIN

▶ *How had some of God's people behaved? (v18–19, 21)*

▶ *So what would God do? (v22)*

▶ *What did God promise to His people?*
v23:
v24:

God's gathering of His people would mean weeding out any who'd never obeyed Him (v18–19). And God would raise up another like David, a great servant of God, to rule and care for His true people. This was pointing forward to Jesus, who would be an even better king than David.

👁 Read verses 25–31

▶ *What else did God promise?*
v25:
v26–27:
v28:

▶ *What truth should God's people cling on to? (v30–31)*

God would send Jesus to rescue His people. Everyone who follows the Good Shepherd can expect a great, secure future. Our present life will be tough and Christians can expect to be attacked. But believers can look forward to a wonderful future of safety (v25), loads of blessings (v26), fruitfulness (v27), rescue (v28), peace and prosperity (v29). And best of all, life in God's presence (v30–31).

PRAY ABOUT IT

Thank God for sending the perfect Shepherd, Jesus. Now look over v25–31, praising and thanking God for each aspect of the great future He promises.

→ TAKE IT FURTHER

Check out Jesus' words on page 119.

54　A new heart

Are you enjoying part 3 of Ezekiel? As well as the usual warnings of judgment (Edom's in for it this time), we keep glimpsing God's amazing promises about His people's fantastic future.

👁 Skim Ezekiel 35 v 1 – 36 v 7

ENGAGE YOUR BRAIN

▷ What was Edom's crime? (35 v 5, 10–13)

▷ What were the consequences? (v6–9)

Edom (descended from Esau) was an old enemy of Israel (descended from Jacob, Esau's brother). Edom waded in and looted Jerusalem when it was conquered (v5). God's punishment would exactly fit Edom's crime — horrifying carnage (v8).

👁 Skim read Ezekiel 36 v 8–38

▷ What did God promise His people? (8–12)

▷ How had they behaved, historically? (v17–18)

▷ What motivated God to rescue His people? (v22–23)

▷ What else would God do for them?
v25:
v26–27:
v29–30:

▷ What effect would all this have? (v31–32)

When God's people were scattered all over the place, their enemies mocked them. "Their God must be weak to let that happen." Now God would bring His people home so the world would know He's a God of power, justice and holiness.

THINK IT OVER

There's great hope for God's people. He gives them a new start, a new heart, a desire to obey Him, and His Spirit to help them do it.

▷ Are you living the life of someone who's been changed by God?

→ TAKE IT FURTHER

The heart of the matter — page 119.

55 | Skeleton army

Ezekiel's message is hope-filled — promises of new leadership, a restored land, rebuilt cities, people with a Spirit-given desire and power to serve God. But how could this happen for a nation that was almost dead?

👁 Read Ezekiel 37 v 1–14

▷ What was Ezekiel's next vision? (v1–2)

▷ What happened? (v7–10)

▷ What was the current attitude of God's people? (v11)

▷ What was God's message to them? (v12–14)

Like a resurrection from the dead. Being rescued from a death-like existence in Babylon, to life as God's people again. Only God can bring life (through the Holy Spirit) to people who deserve the death penalty.

👁 Read verses 15–28

▷ What was God's next task for Ezekiel? (v16–17)

▷ What did it illustrate? (v21–22)

▷ What future did God promise?
v23:
v24:

v25–27:

Incredible. From a disobedient and almost dead nation, God promised to grow a people who would serve Him and live with Him for ever. These promises are coming true already. By His Spirit, God lives among Christians. And one day, He'll do that in person!

PRAY ABOUT IT

Revived. Restored. Reunited perfectly under one King. God promised it. And, one day, He'll complete what He's promised.

▷ How does a chapter like this give us real hope?

Celebrate that real hope now as you talk to God in prayer.

→ TAKE IT FURTHER

No *Take it further* today.

56 Gog smacked

Now for a scary couple of chapters focusing on the mysterious Gog. Gog's only other Bible mention is in Revelation. It seems Gog represents all of God's enemies ganging up on His people. Get ready for God vs Gog.

👁 Read Ezekiel 38 v 1–23

ENGAGE YOUR BRAIN

- ▶ What would God's enemies do? (v8–12)
- ▶ Who was behind this attack on Israel? (v16)
- ▶ What would it lead to? (v18–22)
- ▶ what would be the result? (v23)

👁 Skim read Ezekiel 39 v 1–20

- ▶ What would happen to God's enemies? (v2–6)
- ▶ Why? (v7)
- ▶ What does God call Himself? (v1, 5, 8, 10, 12, 17, 20)

God would send Gog against His (God's) own people, so that He (God) could obliterate His enemies once and for all. Then wild birds would feed on the dead bodies of Gog's guys. Yuk. And it would take 7 months to clear up the carnage. God is sovereign — He's in control. Of everything.

👁 Read verses 21–29

- ▶ What would people realise?
  v22:
  v23:
- ▶ Why did God punish His own people? (v24)
- ▶ But what did the future hold for God's people? (v25–29)

In Revelation, Gog and Magog are used as a warning of all the trouble and opposition Christians will face. But God's telling His people through Ezekiel that they're on the winning side. We need to know this too. And we need to remember it when the world tempts us to not believe it.

PRAY ABOUT IT

Thank God that He's in complete control. Thank Him that even when we face opposition, we can trust that Jesus has already won the victory.

→ TAKE IT FURTHER

Revelation on page 120.

57 Temple vision

God promised to live among His people again, in a restored Israel (37 v 26–27). The last 9 chapters of Ezekiel focus on this great future. So get ready for a vision of God's house — the temple.

👁 Read Ezekiel 40 v 1–4

ENGAGE YOUR BRAIN

▶ *When was this vision? (v1)*

▶ *Where was Ezekiel taken? (v2)*

▶ *What was he told to do? (v4)*

▶ *What did Ezekiel see? (Skim v5–37)*

👁 Read verses 38–43

▶ *What were these rooms used for?*

This all seems very detailed and not very relevant to us! But this was God promising to live among His people again. Talk of sacrifices reminds us that Jesus sacrificed His own life so that our sins could be forgiven. Believers no longer need to go to a temple to be put right with God. We can go straight to God because of Jesus' death and resurrection.

👁 Read Ezekiel 41 v 1–4

"The Most Holy Place" was (obviously) the most special place in God's temple. It symbolised where God lived with His people. Only the high priest was allowed in there, and only once a year, on the Day of Atonement — the day he made sacrifices for people's sins. When Jesus died, the barrier to this room was destroyed. Now Jesus is the only way to God. Anyone can be close to God if they trust in Jesus.

PRAY ABOUT IT

Thank God that He will live with His people for ever. Spend time thanking Him for all that Jesus has achieved for you. Thank God that, through the Holy Spirit, He's present in Christians lives right now, helping them to live for Him in this world.

→ TAKE IT FURTHER

There's more on page 120.

58 ¦ What a comeback!

Way back in chapter 10, we witnessed Jerusalem's misery as God's glory left the temple. It was a tragic moment for God's people. Now it's time for a reversal of fortune.

👁 Read Ezekiel 43 v 1–12

ENGAGE YOUR BRAIN

▶ *What amazing thing did Ezekiel see? (v2–4)*

▶ *What was the brilliant news for God's people? (v5)*

▶ *What did God promise? (v7)*

▶ *What did He demand? (v9)*

God would return to live among His people! Their disobedience and sin had driven God away (v7). Now He expects their devotion and holiness (v9). It's the same for everyone. If we reject God and His ways, we can expect to be separated from Him. But trust and devotion are the right response to God's grace and to living for Him. Throw out the bad stuff.

👁 Read verses 13–27

▶ *What had to happen when someone sinned?*
v19–21:
v22–24:
v25–26:

▶ *What was the result? (v27)*

Blood had to be spilled for sins to be forgiven. It seems weird and a little disgusting. But not even close to how disgusting our sin is to God. You may have noticed we don't offer sacrifices any more. Jesus spilled His blood for us — dying on the cross as the ultimate sacrifice for our sins. The final sacrifice.

PRAY ABOUT IT

What do you need to tell God today? What do you need to thank Him for?

→ TAKE IT FURTHER

No *Take it further* today.

59

Your holiness

Ezekiel's in the middle of one of his spectacular visions. He's looking at God's new temple and God's glory returning to His people. Ezekiel gets a glimpse of God's perfection and holiness. Breathtaking.

👁 Read Ezekiel 44 v 1–14

ENGAGE YOUR BRAIN

▶ *Who's the only one who would have access to God? (v3)*

▶ *What did Ezekiel see and how did it affect him? (v4)*

▶ *How had the Israelites mistreated God's temple? (v7–8)*

▶ *How had the temple servants (Levites) let God down? (v10)*

▶ *Yet how did God show His compassion? (v14)*

God is so holy and perfect that access to Him was severely restricted. When Ezekiel saw God's glory, he fell face down on the floor. We must never forget how amazing, powerful and holy God is.

▶ *Do you give God the respect He deserves?*

▶ *How does your attitude to God need to change?*

👁 Read verses 15–31

▶ *What was the reward for the priests who'd stayed faithful to God? (v15–16)*

▶ *What rules must they follow? (v17–27)*

▶ *What was their biggest reward? (v28–30)*

God is holy and expects His people to live for Him. Those priests who'd obeyed Him would get to serve Him in the temple. They had to follow rules so they were pure enough to serve God. They wouldn't be given land — serving God was reward enough. God expects all believers to stay pure for Him, living His way, longing to serve Him. It's actually an amazing privilege to work for God!

PRAY ABOUT IT

Talk to God about areas of your life where you struggle to stay pure and faithful to Him. Ask for His help in living for Him, serving Him and actually enjoying it!

→ TAKE IT FURTHER

Leave it to Levites on page 120.

60 ¦ Land and sacrifice ¦

God is still showing Ezekiel a vision of His temple when He's back among His people. Look out for another appearance from the mysterious prince, who seems to stand for godly leaders of God's people.

👁 **Read Ezekiel 45 v 1–12**

ENGAGE YOUR BRAIN

▷ *Who gets the best of the land? (v1)*

▷ *How will it be used? (v2–5)*

▷ *What are Israel's leaders ordered to do? (v9)*

Rightly, the best land is given to God, His temple and His servants. No longer will rulers steal land from people or charge high taxes. The new age will be one of justice and fairness.

👁 **Skim read 45 v 13 – 46 v 24**

▷ *What must people give to the prince? (45 v 13–15)*

▷ *How would he use them? (v15)*

▷ *What else must happen? (v18–19)*

▷ *Why? (v20)*

In these detailed chapters, we've been given a glimpse of a future temple and its workings. Everything is designed for organised and reverent worship of God. We've seen that God is so holy that access to Him was majorly restricted. Loads of sacrifices were needed, showing how hugely sinful people are. But God's plans went much further than just a temple. In the end, access to Him would mean the sacrifice of His own Son.

PRAY ABOUT IT

"But now he has appeared once for all at the end of the ages to do away with sin by the sacrifice of himself" (Hebrews 9 v 26). "Therefore, since we are receiving a kingdom that cannot be shaken, let us be thankful, and so worship God acceptably with reverence and awe, for our 'God is a consuming fire'." (Hebrews 12 v 28–29).

→ **TAKE IT FURTHER**
Get some more on page 120.

61 | Let it flow

This is it — we've reached the end of Ezekiel's book of wild visions. His most recent vision was of a new temple brought alive by the presence of God. And now it seems to have sprung a leak.

Read Ezekiel 47 v 1–12

ENGAGE YOUR BRAIN

▷ What was coming out of the temple? (v1)

▷ What shows it brought life? (v7, 9–10)

▷ And healing? (v12)

This beautiful description reminds us of the Garden of Eden. One day, God's people will be restored to a perfect relationship with Him. This river is a picture of God's great blessings for His people — He will give Christians everything they need. Healing. Fruitfulness. True life.

Skim through 47v13 – 48v29

God gave out parts of the land to different people. It was all done with fairness, justice and equality. And that's how God expects us to handle business. Not grabbing for ourselves.

Read Ezekiel 48 v 30–35

▷ What will be the new name of the city? (v35)

After the horror of judgment, God would return to live with His people. Like the river, He'd flood them with blessings. Years later, a new temple *was* built in Jerusalem. But the new temple shows us that Ezekiel's temple pic looks far beyond that to Jesus. He's God's blessing to the world.

THINK IT OVER

Ezekiel's shown God in action to ensure that He's recognised and honoured as the one true God. The God who rules. So face this — it's only as we know God that we can know hope.

▷ How has Ezekiel the book changed your perspective?

▷ In what way has it helped you know God better?

→ TAKE IT FURTHER

Final fix of Ezekiel on page 120.

62 | PSALMS: Praise the Lord!

"Praise the Lord!" It's a bit of a Christian cliché. It's probably made you squirm when you've heard someone shout it or add "PTL!" to the end of a text. But it's a great and important command and something we forget to do.

👁 Read Psalm 111

ENGAGE YOUR BRAIN

▷ *So, what sparked the writer to praise God loads? Jot down (including the verses)...*

What God's done

What God keeps doing for His people

What God's actions tell us about Him

GET ON WITH IT

▷ *If God is like this, what's the best way to respond? (Use v2, 4, 5, 10)*

Verse 10 claims that "the fear of the Lord is the beginning of wisdom".

▷ *How does living God's way show real wisdom?*

▷ *How do you need to be "wiser"?*

THE BOTTOM LINE

Since God is the Creator and Ruler, respect Him (v10a).

Since God is holy, awesome and good, obey Him (v10b).

Since God is like this, praise Him (v10c).

→ TAKE IT FURTHER
Find wisdom on page 121.

TOOLBOX

Quotes and allusions

Each issue, TOOLBOX gives you tips, tools and advice for wrestling with the Bible. This issue, we look at **quotations and allusions**.

QUOTATIONS

Here are two of my favourite quotes:

"I'm not afraid to die. I just don't want to be there when it happens." (Woody Allen)

"The word 'good' has many meanings. For example, if a man were to shoot his grandmother at a range of 500 yards, I'd call him a good shot, but not necessarily a good man." (GK Chesterton)

The Bible uses quotations loads. Usually it's quoting from other parts of the Bible. Later writers (eg: Paul) may quote earlier writers (eg: Moses) to explain or back up what they're saying. It's always a good idea to look up the original quote to check out the context and see exactly what it was actually talking about. Most Bibles will give you the original passage in a footnote.

WHAT'S THE LINK?

Here's an example of quoting from John's account of the crucifixion.

Now it was the day of Preparation, and the next day was to be a special Sabbath. Because the Jews did not want the bodies left on the crosses during the Sabbath, they asked Pilate to have the legs broken and the bodies taken down. The soldiers therefore came and broke the legs of the first man who had been crucified with Jesus, and then those of the other. But when they came to Jesus and found that he was already dead, they did not break his legs. Instead, one of the soldiers pierced Jesus' side with a spear, bringing a sudden flow of blood and water. The man who saw it has given testimony, and his testimony is true. He knows that he tells the truth, and he testifies so that you also may believe. These things happened so that the scripture would be fulfilled: "Not one of his bones will be broken," and, as another scripture says, "They will look on the one they have pierced." (John 19 v 31–37)

What's so special about these quotes? Well, the first one is from Exodus 12 v 46, talking about the Passover lamb that was sacrificed to save the firstborn sons of the Israelites. Jesus' death is the true sacrifice that saves His people from God's judgment.

The second quote comes from Zechariah 12 v 10. If you read the next few verses, you'll get to: *"On that day a fountain will be opened to the house of David and the inhabitants of Jerusalem, to cleanse them from sin and impurity."* (Zechariah 13 v 1). John is using Zechariah to tell us that, on the day Jesus is pierced and dies, it's as though a fountain is opened to wash us clean of all our sin.

ALLUSIONS

Allusions are often harder to spot than quotations as there's nothing explicit to tell you that another part of the Bible is being referred to.

"A man planted a vineyard. He put a wall around it, dug a pit for the winepress and built a watchtower. Then he rented the vineyard to some farmers and went away on a journey." (Mark 12 v 1)

If you were a first-century Jew, you'd immediately think: 'He's picking up the language of Isaiah chapter 5!' But most of us don't know the O.T. well enough to spot allusions. A cross-reference Bible will get you off the hook, but there's no substitute for getting to know your Bible much better. Following a "Read the Bible in a Year" plan will help, and you'll soon start spotting connections between different bits.

REAL OR FAKE?

Use of the same word or idea by two Bible authors doesn't necessarily mean there's a connection. For instance, the fact that Jesus rode into Jerusalem on a donkey (John 12 v 14) is entirely unrelated to Samson killing many men with the jawbone of a donkey (Judges 15). But it *is* related to the prophecy in Zechariah 9 v 9, which John quotes.

So, how can you tell if an allusion is real or not? A general rule of thumb is that the more specific or weird the phrase, the more likely the two are linked. If sheep are mentioned in two places, it's no big deal. But the phrase "sheep without a shepherd" is unusual enough to suggest that both Mark 6 v 34 and Numbers 27 v 17 are linked. Happy quote and allusion spotting!

Ideas taken from Dig Deeper, by Nigel Beynon and Andrew Sach (IVP) available at www.thegoodbook.co.uk

Esther

God's beauty queen

"There I was, on the beach in Spain, and who taps me on the shoulder? Sally from next door! What a coincidence!" Ever wondered why things happen the way they do? Ever been baffled at God's ways? Ever been amazed at seemingly chance occurrences that have tranformed situations?

The book of Esther is full of "coincidences". Esther's twisty, turny story not only tells *what* is happening but gives us some huge clues as to *why* it's happening.

In 539BC, God enabled His people (the Jews) to return to Jerusalem after the punishment of being exiled far from home. Just as He promised in Ezekiel! Some did return (see Ezra and Nehemiah), but others remained, scattered across the Persian empire.

Pretty girl **Esther** was one of them. So was her cousin **Mordecai**. They lived under the rule of Persian King **Xerxes**, his wife **Vashti** and the soon-to-be-appointed prime minister, **Haman**. By now it was the mid-fifth century BC.

This book, Esther, will help us understand God better — His greatness, His plans and the way He works. And so Esther will help us live that bit better for Christ. Get ready, coincidences are about to happen.

63 | Vashti vanishes

Are you ready for a tale of mystery and intrigue with lots of cliffhangers? Well, the story opens with a lavish party in the court of Xerxes, king of all Persia.

☁ Read Esther 1 v 1–9

ENGAGE YOUR BRAIN

▶ *How powerful was Xerxes? (v1)*

▶ *What were the signs of his wealth and extravagance?*
v4:
v6:
v7–8:
v9:

☁ Read verses 10–22

▶ *What was Xerxes' drunken command? (v11)*

▶ *What surprise did he get? (v12)*

▶ *How did he react? (v12–13)*

▶ *What decision was made? (v19)*

▶ *Why? (v19–21)*

Xerxes was drunk and showing off. He wanted everyone to see how gorgeous his queen was. Understandably, she didn't want to be gawped at by the king's drunken mates. Xerxes' furious temper kicked in and the rest is history. His drunkenness, pride and anger led to bad decisions and divorce.

GET ON WITH IT

▶ *Ever had your decisions clouded by alcohol?*

▶ *Ever done something rash when you were angry?*

▶ *What do you need to say sorry to God about?*

▶ *And what relationships do you need to mend that were broken in a rash moment?*

Talk to God about your answers.

THE BOTTOM LINE

Anger and alcohol can get the better of us.

→ TAKE IT FURTHER

Anger and alcohol on page 121.

79

64 ¦ What a beauty!

King Xerxes has dumped his beautiful wife and wants a new queen. What could all this possibly have to do with God and His people?

👁 Read Esther 2 v 1–11

ENGAGE YOUR BRAIN

▶ What was the queen-finding plan? (v2–4)

▶ What coincidences followed? (v5–9)

▶ What was Esther's secret? (v5, 10)

Imagine Esther's mixed feelings when she was chosen as a possible future queen. She would get to live in the king's palace but she would have to leave Mordecai and pretend not to be one of God's people, the Israelites.

It seems unlikely that God would be working through a beauty contest. But He often uses the least likely things and most surprising people in His perfect plans.

👁 Read verses 12–20

▶ What was in store for the girls in the king's harem? (v12–14)

▶ What was special about Esther? (v16–17)

▶ So what happened? (v17–18)

Esther's life would change loads as queen. But she wouldn't forget cousin Mordecai and the way he'd taught her to live. She may be queen now, but she was still one of God's special people — a Jew.

THINK IT OVER

▶ You may or may not be stunningly attractive. But what has God given you the ability to do?

▶ How can you use this gift to serve God?

PRAY ABOUT IT

Thank God that He's in control. Ask Him to use your abilities in His great plans.

→ TAKE IT FURTHER

Why no mention of God? Page 121.

65 | The plot thickens

The twisty turny tale of Esther continues to twist and turn today. We'll uncover two plots: one to murder the king and one to wipe out a whole people.

👁 Read Esther 2 v 21–23

ENGAGE YOUR BRAIN

▷ *What did Mordecai discover? (v21)*

▷ *What dd he do about it? (v22)*

▷ *What happened? (v23)*

Yet another "coincidence" in Esther's story. This little incident will have significance later in the story.

👁 Read Esther 3 v 1–15

▷ *Who became a big shot? (v1)*

▷ *Who refused to bow down to him? (v2)*

▷ *Why do you think he refused?*

▷ *What was Haman's shocking reaction? (v5–6)*

▷ *What law did Haman persuade King Xerxes to make? (v13)*

▷ *How long before it would happen? (v12, 13)*

Haman wasn't satisfied with the idea of killing Mordecai, he wanted to wipe out all of God's people, the Jews. Notice he didn't mention them by name to the king (v8), so he could sneak through his murderous plot.

In countries such as Nepal, Sudan, Syria and Pakistan, Christians are still attacked and even killed. And even if you don't face death for being a Christian, you can expect people to treat you badly for following Jesus.

PRAY ABOUT IT

Pray for Christians in countries where people are imprisoned, attacked or killed for loving Jesus. Ask God to give them the courage to keep living His way, so that many people turn to Jesus in those countries.

→ TAKE IT FURTHER

Keep plotting on page 121.

66 | Getting the sack(cloth)

Esther's cousin Modecai refused to bow down to powerful Haman. So Haman persuaded King Xerxes to issue a decree that all Jews in the kingdom would be slaughtered at the end of the year. Genocide.

👁 Read Esther 4 v 1–8

ENGAGE YOUR BRAIN

▶ How did Mordecai and the Jews respond to the news? (v1–3)

▶ What did Mordecai want Esther to do? (v8)

People wore sackcloth and ashes to show they were massively upset. Sackcloth was made of rough goats' hair. Ashes were the black bits left after a fire. Uncomfortable stuff! But there was hope for God's people. Mordecai realised that God had put someone in a position to help them.

👁 Read verses 9–17

▶ Why didn't Esther want to approach the king? (v11)

▶ What did Mordecai say?
v13:
v14:

▶ What was Esther's answer and what did she request? (v16)

Esther was worried she'd be killed for just approaching the king. But Mordecai knew she'd been made queen for a reason and there was nothing to lose. Eventually, Esther agreed and asked that all the Jews go without food for 3 days to pray for her.

GET ON WITH IT

Sometimes, fear can lead us to do nothing rather than take a risk for God. For example, chickening out of telling friends about Jesus' impact on your life. But really, what do you have to lose? Take a leaf out of Esther's book, take a chance and ask Christian friends to pray for you.

PRAY ABOUT IT

Ask God to help you serve Him in the situation He's put you in. Ask Him for courage to do what you know you should do. Then message friends to pray for you.

➔ TAKE IT FURTHER

More wise words on page 122.

67 | Gallows humour

Tense stuff. Esther, Mordecai and the Jews in Susa went without food and prayed their sandals off (4 v 15–17). But would Esther chicken out? Would Haman succeed? Would God's people be wiped from the map? Would Esther die?

👁 Read Esther 5 v 1–8

ENGAGE YOUR BRAIN

ⓘ *What was the first positive sign for Esther? (v2)*

ⓘ *And the second? (v3)*

ⓘ *What did Esther request? (v4)*

ⓘ *When her chance came, what did she ask for? (v8)*

What suspense! Esther has had two opportunities to beg for her people's lives, but so far she's just handed out dinner invitations! What will happen?

👁 Read verses 9–14

ⓘ *What was Haman's view of himself? (v11)*

ⓘ *What did he think of Esther's invitation? (v12)*

ⓘ *What made him furious? (v9, 13)*

ⓘ *So what did he do? (v14)*

Everything's in the balance for God's people. The king has ordered all Jews to be put to death. Their hope now rests on Queen Esther's shoulders. But so far, she hasn't got around to even telling King Xerxes that she's a Jew. Things are not looking good. And now Haman has built a huge gallows to hang Mordecai.

Only God can bring rescue to such a hopeless situation. All humans are in a desperate situation — sinful and awaiting God's death sentence. But God Himself has arranged for the rescue — Jesus alone can save us from the death sentence.

PRAY ABOUT IT

Talk to God about anything tough you're facing at the moment. Thank Him for His power and His compassion. Thank Him for the rescue He offers though Jesus.

→ TAKE IT FURTHER

No *Take it further* today.

68 Robe reversal

Haman's feeling smug because he's the king's favourite. Everything seems to be going well for him — and he's soon going to kill his enemy Mordecai and all the Jews. But one sleepless night was about to change everything.

Read Esther 6 v 1–9

ENGAGE YOUR BRAIN

▶ *What did Xerxes discover in the history book? (v2–3)*

▶ *What did Haman think the king wanted to do? (v6)*

▶ *So what did he suggest? (v7–9)*

So far, Haman's hopes were high. He thought Xerxes was going to honour him, not Mordecai! If the king was ready to do all this for Haman, then Mordecai's death was a small thing to ask for! But God was turning Haman's plans inside out.

Read verses 10–14

▶ *What was the twist in the tale for Haman? (v10)*

▶ *What did he have to do for his hated enemy? (v11)*

▶ *How did it affect Haman? (v12)*

▶ *What did his wife and advisers tell him? (v13)*

▶ *What would happen next? (v14)*

Loads more "coincidences" today. God was at work behind the scenes. Just at the right time, God reminded King Xerxes of what Mordecai had done for him. Haman thought he would get revenge on Mordecai, but he had his hopes dashed by God's perfect timing. Amazing.

PRAY ABOUT IT

Have little coincidences ever caused things to work out just right for you? Thank God for any times you've seen Him use "coincidences" to work out His perfect plan in your life.

→ TAKE IT FURTHER

Coincidentally, there's more to be found on page 122.

69 The big banquet

Oh, the unbearable tension. What would happen at Esther's banquet? Would Mordecai be strung up? Would Esther ask the BIG question? Would God's people survive? Who needs soaps when you've got this nail-biting drama?

Read Esther 7 v 1–10

ENGAGE YOUR BRAIN

- What did the king ask Esther yet again? (v2)
- How did she answer this time? (v3–4)
- Who was revealed as the villain of the story? (v6)
- How did the king respond? (v7)
- How about Haman? (v7)
- How did he make things even worse for himself? (v8)
- What was ironic about his fate? (v9–10)

Once again, the whole story is turned on its head. Haman seemed to be flavour of the month and was close to wiping out his enemy Mordecai and all of the Jews in the kingdom. But Esther finally admitted her Jewish roots in a moving speech. King Xerxes was furious he'd been tricked into ordering the extermination of his wife's people, so Haman would pay for his plotting. Egotistical Haman had hoped to hang Mordecai from the huge gallows he built. Instead, it was his own body that hung from a great height.

GET ON WITH IT

Proverbs 26 v 27 fits perfectly. Check it out and then memorise it.

THINK IT OVER

- Ever plan to bring someone down?
- Is there someone you deliberately hurt?

PRAY ABOUT IT

Talk to God about these things. Ask Him to help you make peace with your enemies. Or family who wind you up until you treat them badly.

Haman was hanged. But the law to kill all the Jews still stood. And Xerxes *never* changed his laws. While Haman hung on the gallows, Jewish lives hung in the balance.

→ TAKE IT FURTHER
More coincidences on page 122.

70 | Celebration nation

Haman is hanged. Esther and Mordecai are safe. But there's a problem. The law to destroy all the Jews still stands. And King Xerxes isn't allowed to change his laws.

👁 Read Esther 8 v 1–8

ENGAGE YOUR BRAIN

▷ *What did King Xerxes do for Esther? (v1)*

▷ *And for Mordecai? (v2)*

▷ *What did Esther again beg the king for? (v3–6)*

▷ *What was the problem? (end of v8)*

Xerxes had ordered that all the Jews be slaughtered on the thirteenth day of the twelfth month. This law couldn't be changed. But another law could be made...

👁 Read verses 9–17

▷ *What new law was passed? (v11–12)*

▷ *How did the Jews react? (v16–17)*

▷ *How did it affect other people? (end of v17)*

The law to attack the Jews still stood, but now they could defend themselves. So only their enemies would attack them, not everyone, as King Xerxes was now on their side. All of this led to more people joining God's people, the Jews (v17).

They weren't safe yet, but the Jews certainly thought everything would be OK (v16). So they celebrated something that hadn't yet happened. We can do the same. God has promised to rescue His people. This life will be hard for Christians, but one day Jesus will return and gather His followers for a perfect eternity. That's worth celebrating!

PRAY ABOUT IT

Spend time thanking God for some of His promises that have yet to be fulfilled. And think how you can share your joy over a brilliant future promised by God.

→ TAKE IT FURTHER

Parallel universe on page 122.

71 Day of destruction

The time has come — it's destroy or be destroyed.
What would happen on the 13th day of the 12th
month? Execution of God's people? Or them beating
up the rest?

Read Esther 9 v 1–10

ENGAGE YOUR BRAIN

▶ What did happen? (v1–2)

▶ What did politicians do? (v3)

▶ How had life changed for
Mordecai? (v4)

▶ What happened to the enemies
of God's people? (v5–10)

Read verses 11–17

▶ What extra request did Esther
make? (v13)

▶ What fact is repeated in verses
10, 15 and 16?

▶ What happened after all the
fighting? (v17)

It was a day drenched in blood.
75,000 people were killed. Horrific.
But this was God's day of punishment
for everyone who had been against
His people. That's why the Jews had

to kill so many. God was protecting
His people and protecting His
enemies. Maybe that explains why
Esther asked for another day to kill
more of their enemies.

A day is coming when God will fight
against everyone who is still on the
wrong side. Everyone who has not
trusted in Jesus to save them will be
punished. And all of God's people
will be rescued from sin and death.
No more sadness or pain.

PRAY ABOUT IT

Think of 5 people you know who
are God's enemies. People who hate
Christianity, or maybe are positive
about it but won't accept Jesus as
their King. Ask God to bring about
an incredible U-turn in their lives.

→ TAKE IT FURTHER

Check out God's plans on page 122.

72 | Party!

God's people, the Jews, didn't get wiped out! In fact, their enemies were the ones who suffered. Time for a party!

👁 Read Esther 9 v 18–32

ENGAGE YOUR BRAIN

▶ *What did Mordecai make sure happened? (v20–22)*

▶ *Why was it called Purim (the pur was a lot / dice thing)? (v23–26)*

▶ *What did they do at Purim? (v22, 27–28)*

The Jews' happiness bubbled over to others. They had been rescued from their enemies, and they showed their thanks to God in a practical way by giving to other people. They didn't celebrate this occasion just once, but every year. Esther and Mordecai made sure that God's people would never forget God's goodness to them.

👁 Read Esther 10 v 1–3

▶ *How would you describe Mordecai's status?*

▶ *Why was he so popular?*

Well, that's the Esther story. A miraculous reversal of situations, celebrated with a festival. At the beginning, Esther was an unknown, pretty Jewish girl, stuck in a foreign country. At the end, she's the powerful queen of Persia, who helped save God's people. At the start, Mordecai was a hated Jew who was going to be hanged. Now he's Prime Minister. The second most powerful man in the country.

God isn't mentioned in Esther, but He's clearly behind the scenes for His people and for His own glory. In Esther's pages we glimpse God's character, His promises, His power and His providence.

PRAY ABOUT IT

Thank God that He rescues His people. Thank Him that He's in control of everything. Ask Him to help you serve Him and serve His people.

→ TAKE IT FURTHER

The after party is on page 122.

73 | Psalms: The good life

Time for a trio of psalms over the next three days. What's it mean to live a godly life? Psalm 112 paints a positive picture of a life lived for God.

⊙ Read Psalm 112

ENGAGE YOUR BRAIN

▷ *How is this man described?*
v1:
v4:
v5:
v9:

▷ *What was the result for him?*
v2:
v3:
v5:
v6–8:

▷ *What about the person who doesn't live for God? (v10)*

The Christian is life is *not* perfect. There will be times of sadness and stress. But a life lived for God *is* full of blessing. God hasn't promised to give us everything we *want*, but He'll make sure His people have everything they *need*.

When we come to trust in Jesus, we're given His "righteousness" — being right with God (v3). And so we're to grow in righteousness, becoming more like God.

This psalm gives us examples of what this will involve.
• A reverence for God (v1).
• A delight in obeying Him (v1).
• Upright/moral living (v2).
• Outgoing care for others (v4).
• A don't-think-twice generosity (v5, 9).
• Acting with fairness (v5).

GET ON WITH IT

▷ *Which of these areas do you need to work on?*

▷ *So what exactly will you do about it this week?*

PRAY ABOUT IT

Read verses 5–9, asking God to help you become more like the person described here.

→ TAKE IT FURTHER

More top tips on page 123.

74 Glory to God

Think about this question — what makes God worth shouting about? Can you come up with any good answers? This psalm should give you some ideas.

Read Psalm 113 v 1–6

ENGAGE YOUR BRAIN

▷ What should believers do? (v1–2)

▷ When? (v2–3)

▷ Why should God be praised constantly?
v4:
v5–6:

God's so great, He even has to stoop down to look at the heavens and earth! He's the King. The boss. In control of everything. He's glorious. So we should sing and shout about Him. Loads.

Read verses 7–9

▷ What does our glorious God do for the weak, poor and needy?

God looks after those who need His help. He cares for people we'd probably ignore or look down on. By the way, v9 isn't a promise that God will give all childless women a baby.

It's more a guarantee that God does draw near to care for His people in the way that's best for us.

GET ON WITH IT

▷ If that's how God treats people in need, how should we?

▷ Who do you need to stop ignoring?

▷ Who will you show God's love to? And how?

SHARE IT

Verse 5 asks: "Who is like the Lord?"

▷ What would you say?

▷ How can you explain God's greatness in a simple, enthusiastic way?

THE BOTTOM LINE

Praise the Lord. Right now!

→ TAKE IT FURTHER

See God in action on page 123.

75 | Time to tremble

Yesterday we found reasons to shout about God. Well, this psalm gives us specific examples of God's greatness and uniqueness. (By the way, Judah, Israel and Jacob are all names for God's Old Testament people.)

👁 **Read Psalm 114 v 1–4**

ENGAGE YOUR BRAIN

▷ What event in history is this psalm talking about?

▷ What's amazing about v2?

In Exodus, God brought His people throught the Red Sea (no wet feet) and later across the Jordan into the promised land. Think what it took for God to rescue His people like this — manouevring nations and commanding His creation. Amazing.

Most incredibly of all, all-powerful God shared His presence with His people (v2), living among them. So there was no room for treating God casually or dismissing Him.

👁 **Read verses 5–8**

▷ What do v5–6 tell us about God?

▷ What's the right response to such a powerful God? (v7)

God used His power to benefit His (often sinful) people, providing for them on the way to the promised land (v8). Today, we look back on the cross of Jesus as the ultimate example of God providing for us. Think how God has used His power to bring so many benefits to everyone who trusts Him.

PRAY ABOUT IT

It's time to make the right response to God.

→ **TAKE IT FURTHER**

Explore the Old Testament on page 123.

76 | Matthew: Are you ready?

We're back in Matthew, near the end of Jesus' life. Before you read this next section, remember that this really happened. It really happened to the Son of God. Don't just read the words — feel the emotions.

👁 Read Matthew 26 v 36–44

ENGAGE YOUR BRAIN

▶ *How is Jesus feeling? (v37–38)*

▶ *What does He ask His Father God to do? (v39)*

The cup is a picture of God's wrath — His right anger at, and punishment of, sin (see *Take It Further*). To be given this cup is to experience God's judgment. That's what Jesus knows is going to happen to Him as He dies on the cross. Remember that Jesus has never done anything wrong. God has no reason to be angry with Him.

▶ *What is amazing about what Jesus says in v42?*

It's incredible that Jesus would take God's punishment in His friends' place. Especially when we see what His friends are like…

▶ *What does He ask them to do for Him? (v38, 41)*

▶ *How do they react? (v40, 43)*

THINK ABOUT IT

Have you realised how awful the cross was for Jesus? He'd been loved by His Father for all eternity; on the cross, He knew only His Father's anger.

Have you realised that He did this for you? You deserve God's wrath, but Jesus drank your cup.

Have you realised how undeserving you are? You let down Jesus all the time (we all do). He knew that, and still He died for you. Astonishing.

PRAY ABOUT IT

How can you not thank Jesus for all of this?

THE BOTTOM LINE

Jesus drank the horrific cup of God's wrath — for you.

→ TAKE IT FURTHER

More cup stuff on page 123.

77 | Who's in control?

**Does Jesus tell you what your life should be like?
Or do you tell Him?**

Read Matthew 26 v 45–50

Again, it looks on the surface as if everything's out of Jesus' control. And yet it's Jesus who gives Judas permission to betray Him (v50).

Read verses 51–56

ENGAGE YOUR BRAIN

▷ *Draw the scene (doesn't need to be a masterpiece!):*

▷ *What is Jesus' priority? (v54, 56)*

▷ *What is the disciples' priority...*
in v51?
at the end of v56?

Jesus could whistle up an army of tooled-up angels (v53)! But He doesn't. His plan is not to win a military victory, but to defeat death on the cross, just as the prophets predicted in the Old Testament. The disciples don't trust or like Jesus' plan. When He won't fit in with what they want to do, they abandon Him.

THINK ABOUT IT

We all either fit in with Jesus' plan for our lives, even when that's hard — or we try to make Jesus fit in with our plans, and forget about Him when He won't.

How have you done hard things for Jesus in the last month. Praise God and be encouraged!

How have you decided to follow your own plan, and turned your back on Jesus when it's hard? Be challenged and ask God for help!

THE BOTTOM LINE

Follow Jesus' plan, not your own, even when it's hard.

TAKE IT FURTHER

Find a little bit more on page 123.

78 | Who's on trial?

Judas is guilty of betrayal. The disciples are guilty of desertion. Next, it's Jesus on trial. Or is it? As you read, picture the scene in your head, and feel the tension of the conversation.

Read Matthew 26 v 57–64

ENGAGE YOUR BRAIN

▷ How fair is Jesus' trial? (v59–60)

Notice that Jesus doesn't answer the crooked judges about the fake evidence (v63). The chief priests are getting nowhere… so the high priest gets right to the heart of the issue.

▷ What does he challenge Jesus to do? (v63)

▷ How does Jesus answer? What does He add? (v64)

Jesus is guilty of one thing: being the Son of God. And as He stands on trial, He points forward to another trial, when everyone, including His enemies, will see Him "coming on the clouds of heaven".

READ VERSES 65–68

▷ What does the high priest find Jesus guilty of?

▷ What sentence do they pass? (v66)

THINK ABOUT IT

The world still puts Jesus on trial today. It pre-judges Jesus, refuses to listen to Him, and then dismisses Him as a fake. But one day He will judge the world. And the world will have nothing to say (see Romans 3 v 19).

▷ How does this encourage you to keep following Jesus in a world which rejects Him?

GET ON WITH IT

Jesus told the truth about Himself even when on trial for His life. In what situations can you stand up for the truth about Him, even when it risks rejection, unpopularity, or even physical harm? Ask God to give you the courage to actually do this.

→ TAKE IT FURTHER

Trial and error — page 123.

79 | Denied

As Jesus stands in the courtroom, facing death, another man is put on trial just outside.

👁 Read Matthew 26 v 57–58

ENGAGE YOUR BRAIN
▶ *Where is Peter as Jesus' trial begins? (v58)*

👁 Read verses 69–75

Three times Peter is given a chance to stand up for the truth about Jesus.

▶ *What does he do with those chances? (v70, 72, 74).*

▶ *Who is interrogating him? (v69, 71, 73)?*

As Jesus stands up to the most important priest in the whole nation, Peter caves in to two girls and some bystanders. Pathetic!

But unsurprising, because Jesus had said this would happen. He knew Peter, and He knew Peter was flawed and would disown Him (v34).

▶ *When the cock crows, what does Peter remember? (v74–75)*

▶ *How does he react to realising what he's done?*

GET ON WITH IT
We're all Peters. We all fail to stand up for Jesus. We all fail to be loyal to Him in what we say and how we live. But do we all react like Peter? He "wept bitterly". He was honest about himself and what he'd done. He didn't make excuses. He didn't convince himself it didn't matter. He wept.

And the question is: when we let Jesus down, does it affect us as deeply?

PRAY ABOUT IT
Admit to Jesus ways in which you've denied Him. Feel the pain of letting Him down. Then thank Him that He knows all your flaws, and that He still died for you.

→ TAKE IT FURTHER
The next conversation we hear between Peter and Jesus — p123.

80 | Dead end or happy end?

Yesterday we saw Peter in tears when he realised he'd let Jesus down. Today we focus on someone who had even more of a reason for feeling rotten and pathetic.

👁 Read Matthew 27 v 1-4

ENGAGE YOUR BRAIN

Jesus has now been condemned to death (v1–2).

▶ *How does Judas, "who had betrayed him", feel about this? (v3)*

▶ *What does he do, and why? (v3–4)*

He regrets his sin. He confesses his sin. He tries to make up for his sin.

👁 Read verses 5–10

▶ *What does Judas end up doing? (v5)*

Judas was really sorry, just as Peter was. Peter went on to be one of Jesus' main men, preaching the gospel and setting up churches. So why isn't there a happy end to Judas' story? It's because he hasn't done one crucial thing. Let's listen in to Peter preaching, later on, in Acts.

👁 Read Acts 3 v 19–21

▶ *What does he tell people to do? (v19)*

▶ *What will then happen to their sins? (v19)*

Judas knew he'd sinned — but he didn't look to Jesus to wipe them out for him. Instead he tried to make up for them. But he couldn't. And he ended up dead.

Feeling bad about sin, confessing it, and trying to repair the damage is no use if we don't also turn to Jesus as Lord, and ask Him to be our Saviour.

PRAY ABOUT IT

Do you need to "repent and turn to God" and ask him to "wipe out" a particular sin?

→ TAKE IT FURTHER

More background on this tragic story on page 124.

81 God's king? Kill Him!

It's one of the most stupid decisions ever.
Looking at Jesus and saying: "Kill Him".
Why did they do it?

👁 Read Matthew 27 v 11–31

ENGAGE YOUR BRAIN

Three sets of people send "the king of the Jews" (v11) to the cross. Each has a different reason.

The chief priests stand next to Pilate, the Roman governor, accusing Jesus (v12).

🅓 *Why? (v18)?*

In other words, they want to be in charge. They need Jesus out of the way so they can keep their power.

The people

🅓 *What does Pilate ask the crowd? (v17)*
🅓 *What's the sensible answer?*
🅓 *Why do they choose to crucify Jesus? (v20)*

The governor

🅓 *How does Pilate's wife describe Jesus? (v19)*
🅓 *But what does Pilate do? (v26)*

Why? Because he's afraid of an uproar (v24). He does what's easiest, not what's right. He's a coward.

THINK ABOUT IT

We don't shout "Crucify him!" But we do live as though Jesus doesn't exist and isn't King — we sin. And we do it for the same reasons…

When do you reject Jesus as your King because:
• you want to be in charge, not Him?
• you listen to those around you, not Him?
• you choose what's easiest, rather than obeying Him?

THE BOTTOM LINE

Sin is stupid. These people chose not to let God's loving King be part of their lives — and chose to set loose a murderer (Luke 23 v 19). Sin means turning away from the perfect King, choosing to mess things up. Stupid.

→ TAKE IT FURTHER

A little more on page 124.

82 | Loser or Lord?

Who died on the cross? OK, clearly it was Jesus, but who was He, really? Jesus' followers called Him "Lord". Yet many people who saw Jesus die thought He was a pathetic loser.

👁 Read Matthew 27 v 32–44

ENGAGE YOUR BRAIN

Really try to picture the scene.

▶ What do people walking past say to Jesus? (v40)

▶ What would make them believe Jesus is the "Son of God"?

▶ What do the religious leaders say about Jesus? (v42–43)

▶ What would make them believe Jesus is God's King?

But Jesus stays hanging from the cross. And these people look at Him and say: He's a loser. He clearly isn't the Son of God.

But they've totally misunderstood. It's because of who Jesus is that He stays on the cross. If He hadn't been God's Son, He'd never have let Himself be killed without a fight. If He hadn't been God's King, He wouldn't be dying to save people from God's punishment: eternal death.

👁 Read Matthew 27 v 54

▶ What do the Roman soldiers say about Jesus?

As Jesus dies on the cross, these men look at Him and say: He's clearly the Son of God. He is the Lord.

THINK ABOUT IT

When you look at Jesus on the cross, do you see a loser or do you see your Lord?

PRAY ABOUT IT

Thank Jesus that, although He could have easily saved Himself from the cross, He chose not to. Thank Him for deciding to go through all this so that you don't have to.

THE BOTTOM LINE

Jesus isn't a loser — He's our Lord.

→ TAKE IT FURTHER

Cross words on page 124.

83

The big question

**People sometimes ask "Why did Jesus die?"
Actually, He tells us Himself.**

👁 **Read Matthew 27 v 45–46**

ENGAGE YOUR BRAIN
The "sixth hour" (v45) is midday.

▷ *What's strange about what happens in v45?*

Centuries before, God had warned this would be a sign of His anger (Amos 8 v 9). Of course God was furious — His Son was being killed! But the great surprise of the cross is not that God was angry, but who He was angry with…

▷ *What did Jesus shout? (v46)*

"Forsaken" means "abandoned" or "deserted".

▷ *What is the dying Son of God saying about His relationship with His Father?*

The punishment of complete separation from the loving God, from all joy and hope and health, should be falling on the mocking people and gloating leaders. Instead, it's falling

on God's perfect, innocent Son.

👁 **Read verses 47–50**

As He explained why He was dying, Jesus mentioned Eloi — God (v46). But people didn't bother to listen carefully. They thought He'd said Elijah (v47). So they completely failed to understand why Jesus died. People still do that today. They don't listen to God's Son explaining that His death is the only way they can avoid God's punishment of being abandoned by Him for ever.

Are you listening?

PRAY ABOUT IT
The punishment should have fallen on me and you. Instead, it fell on Jesus. He offers to take your place. Have you ever asked Him to do this for you? If not, what's stopping you? If you have, when was the last time you actually thanked Him properly? Do it now!

→ **TAKE IT FURTHER**
There's even more on page 124.

84 | Can people live with God?

You probably don't ask this very often! But it's of eternal importance. If we can't survive in God's presence, we face an eternity cut off from Him and all good things.

ANSWER ONE

👁 Read Genesis 3 v 22–24

▷ *What had humans done? (v22)*

Here, "knowing" means "deciding" — an attempt to become like God, making the rules ourselves. That's sin.

▷ *What would humans no longer be able to do? (v22–23)*
▷ *What was the barrier between God and man? (v24)*

So, can people live with God? NO.

ANSWER TWO

1500 years before Jesus, God told His people that He'd live among them in a tent called the tabernacle. In the centre of this tent was the place God dwelled in all His perfection — the "ark". And God told the people to put a curtain around it.

👁 Read Exodus 26 v 31–33

▷ *How does what is on this curtain link back to Genesis 3?*

The curtain represented the separation between perfect God and sinful people.

Can people live with God? NO.

ANSWER THREE

Eventually, the curtain got moved into the temple.

👁 Read Matthew 27 v 50–56

▷ *As Jesus died, what happened? (v50)*
▷ *What does this show is the great achievement of Jesus' death?*

PRAY ABOUT IT

Thank Jesus that He died for your sin and removed the barrier so you can live with God. Ask Him to give you certainty that you're headed for perfect eternity in God's presence.

THE BOTTOM LINE

Can people live with God? YES.

→ TAKE IT FURTHER

Meet the living dead on page 124.

85 | A real follower

Today's verses show us one way to see if we're true disciples of Jesus, the crucified King.

👁 **Read Matthew 27 v 57–61**

ENGAGE YOUR BRAIN

▶ *What does v57 tell us about Joseph?*

▶ *What does he do? (v58–60)*

Remember that the last thing Pilate did was to have Jesus tortured and killed.

▶ *How is Joseph taking a huge risk in v58, do you think?*

▶ *How is Joseph giving something up for Jesus in v59–60?*

Remember who Joseph's doing all this for — a corpse! Jesus is dead! Surely risking everything for (and giving everything to) Jesus can't do any good now… yet Joseph still does it.

And in the end, Joseph has the great privilege of his tomb being the place where Jesus rose from the dead. But he doesn't know that as he speaks to

Pilate, or lays Jesus' body to rest.

▶ *How is Joseph an example of how a true follower of Jesus acts?*

GET ON WITH IT

▶ *What risks can you take to stand up for Jesus this week?*

▶ *What things can you give to serving Jesus this week — some money? Some time? Some talents? Some words?*

👁 **Read verses 62–66**

The religious leaders wanted to completely crush the "Jesus cult". Instead, they made it certain that, when Jesus' body disappeared from the tomb, it was impossible that His disciples had stolen it.

THE BOTTOM LINE

True Jesus-followers risk everything, and give everything, to Him.

➔ **TAKE IT FURTHER**

No *Take it further* today.

86 Jesus is risen – so what?

Ever seen a sports team snatch victory from the jaws of defeat? Or a film where all seems lost but then the hero makes a spectacular comeback? Today we see the greatest victory, the most amazing comeback, of all time.

👁 Read Matthew 28 v 1–7

ENGAGE YOUR BRAIN

▶ *Sum up in a sentence what happens in verses 1-4:*

▶ *Why is Jesus' dead body not in the tomb? (v6)*

▶ *Who had predicted this would happen? (v6)*

▶ *How do you think you'd have felt if you'd been with the women?*

▶ *What does the resurrection show about Jesus' promises?*

👁 Read verses 8–10

▶ *How are the women feeling? (v8)*

▶ *How do they react to meeting the risen Jesus? (v9)*

▶ *What does He tell them to do? (v10)*

GET ON WITH IT

▶ *How do verses 8–10 show us what the right reactions to Jesus' resurrection are?*
v8:
v9:

▶ *How can you do each of these things this week?*

PRAY ABOUT IT

Thank God that Jesus rose from the dead and that everything He says is true. Thank Him that you can rely completely on Him.

THE BOTTOM LINE

Jesus is risen. This should give us great joy. We should live for Jesus and tell other people about Him.

→ TAKE IT FURTHER

Promises promises on page 124.

87 Killing the truth

Someone you were involved in killing has come back to life. What do you do?!

👁 **Read Matthew 28 v 11–15**

ENGAGE YOUR BRAIN

The chief priests had Jesus executed. Now it seems He's come back to life. Here's their choice: admit they were wrong and take Jesus seriously, or keep ignoring reality.

▷ *What choice do the religious leaders take? (12–14)*

These are professional soldiers — they would never all have fallen asleep (v13)! Ever since that day, no one's come up with a convincing explanation of what happened at Jesus' tomb — apart from that He is the Son of God, risen from the dead.

TALK ABOUT IT

▷ *What reasons do people give for not believing Jesus rose from the dead? Can you answer them?*

If you're not too confident, get together with some Christian friends and practise talking about why you believe in the resurrection.

The chief priests chose to ignore reality and make up a story. But not everyone reacted like that to the crime of killing Jesus…

👁 **Read Acts 2 v 22–23, 37–41**

These men realise they've done something terrible in killing Jesus (v23). They know they need to change (v38). 3000 of them stop opposing Jesus, and instead accept Him as Lord and Saviour (v38, 41).

GET ON WITH IT

It's the same today. People hear they've rejected the risen Jesus, God's Son, and are in trouble. Lots keep ignoring reality. But some realise their sin, and accept Jesus as their Lord and Saviour.

▷ *Who could you talk to about the risen Jesus today?*

→ **TAKE IT FURTHER**

Brilliant news on page 125.

88 | What Jesus deserves

Why should Christians tell other people about Jesus? It can be so difficult, cause us hassle, and leave people thinking we're crazy. Why bother? Well, here's one big reason, straight from the lips of Christ Himself...

Read Matthew 28 v 16–20

ENGAGE YOUR BRAIN

▶ *Where do the disciples go, and who do they meet? (v16–17)*

This shouldn't have surprised them. Jesus had told the women this would happen (v10) — and, as we've seen, what Jesus says will happen always happens.

▶ *What big claim does Jesus make? (v18)*

▶ *So how does Jesus want His followers to respond? (v19–20)*

Because of who Jesus is — the crucified, risen Lord, in charge of absolutely everything — He deserves all people to love Him and respect Him. If we understand who Jesus is, we'll love and respect Him so much that we'll tell others about Him. Because we'll want Him to enjoy their love and respect, too. Jesus is Lord — THEREFORE we should tell others

about Him. But doing this is hard!

That's why the last sentence of Matthew's Gospel is fantastic! Jesus doesn't just send us to tell people about Him — He goes with us as we do it. Awesome.

GET ON WITH IT

▶ *Who are you going to try to tell about how great Jesus is?*

If you find yourself not really wanting to — remember that Jesus is amazing and deserves their love and respect.

PRAY ABOUT IT

Pray for those people now. Thank Jesus that He's with you. Ask Him to give you courage to talk about Him.

THE BOTTOM LINE

Jesus deserves love and respect — THEREFORE tell others about Him.

→ TAKE IT FURTHER

Quick, find out what's on page 125.

89 | Psalms: Why worship?

If someone asked you why you worship God — or why you sing songs in church — what would you say?

👁 Read Psalm 115 v 1

▷ *Who should we make sure gets the glory?*

▷ *Why?*

▷ *And who shouldn't get the praise and glory?*

It's so natural to chase after people's respect and praise. But believers should be ensuring God gets all the honour and glory He deserves. When we succeed in something and are praised, we must point out that God makes it possible.

👁 Read verses 2–8

In Bible times, many people carried idols with them — little statues of gods. They were God-substitutes.

▷ *What sets God apart from idols? (v3)*

▷ *Why is it stupid to trust in dead idols? (v8)*

▷ *What God-substitutes do people have today?*

▷ *What should be the Christian's response to these things?*

👁 Read verses 9–18

▷ *Why should God's people trust in Him? (v9–11)*

▷ *How does He treat His people? (v12–15)*

▷ *What privilege and responsibility has He given them? (v16)*

▷ *What point is v17–18 making?*

God can be fully relied on. And He chooses us to look after the world He's given us. And it's down to us to sing His praises and tell everyone about Him.

GET ON WITH IT

Let's use this week and then our whole lives to make sure God gets honoured. Not ourselves. The opportunity for praising God starts the moment you finish this sentence.

→ TAKE IT FURTHER

Back to the beginning on page 125.

90 | A passionate life

Passion for God. Have you got it? Remember a time when you did? Do you know someone with such a love for God that they can't help talking about Him? Want to be like them? Then ask God to use this psalm to help you.

◉ Read Psalm 116 v 1–11

▶ Why did the writer love God? (v1–4)

▶ How does he describe God? (v5)

▶ How had God treated him? (v6–7)

▶ How would he respond to God rescuing him? (v9)

▶ How could you use v1–9 to explain how God rescues believers from sin and death?

Clearly, the Lord had rescued this guy from his enemies (v10–11) and a near-death experience. He was eternally grateful to God; he recognised God's grace and love; and he resolved to walk God's way (v9).

All Christians have experienced God rescuing them from sin and the road to eternal death. They've seen His grace and compassion in action. And so they want to live God's way from now on.

◉ Read verses 12–19

▶ What does this grateful guy decide to do?
v14:
v16:
v17:

God saved his life, so now he devoted his life to serving God. That's real passion. And the right response to Jesus laying down His life for us is to lay down our own lives for Him as living sacrifices. That means devoting ourselves to living His way because we're so thankful for what He's done for us.

PRAY ABOUT IT

Christians can say: "I love the Lord, for He heard my voice". Ask God to bring out real passion in you so you devote your life to Him.

→ TAKE IT FURTHER

Living sacrifices — page 125.

91 Short and sweet

Psalm 117 is the shortest psalm in the Bible, but it's tasty stuff. It contains a vital command and some simple but powerful truths about God. Worth getting your teeth into.

Read Psalm 117

Now read it again

ENGAGE YOUR BRAIN
▷ What does "extol" mean? (Look it up if you need to.)

Try to sum up the command (v1) and reason for it (v2). Do it in one sentence without using any word that appears in the psalm!

▷ Which O.T. events might have inspired the writer to sing about God's love and faithfulness?

▷ How has God ultimately shown His love and faithfulness to His people?

The psalm-writer knew God had rescued and protected His people many times. Ultimately, God's love and faithfulness were shown on the cross. One day, everyone will acknowledge Jesus as King. Some willingly as His servants, some too late to be rescued from God's punishment. We must decide in this life which we'll be.

THINK IT OVER
▷ What can you praise God for?

▷ How specifically has He shown love and faithfulness to you?

PRAY ABOUT IT
Hopefully, you've got loads to praise and thank God for today.

→ TAKE IT FURTHER
More prayer ideas on page 125.

92 | In the background

Ever looked at a photo or painting long enough to find a background detail getting sharper until it takes over? This psalm is about God's Old Testament people, but look carefully to see someone emerge from the background.

◉ Read Psalm 118 verses 1–9

ENGAGE YOUR BRAIN

ⓓ Why should we thank God? (v1)

ⓓ What did the writer do when he was worried and in trouble? (v5)

ⓓ What's his attitude towards other people? (v6, 8)

ⓓ And towards God? (v6–9)

It's so easy to get weighed down by the worries of this life. And to care too much how others view/treat us. But we should be more concerned with how God views us . And remember He's with us every step of the way, even in the darkest times.

◉ Read verses 10–21

ⓓ What did God do for this guy? (v13–14, 18)

ⓓ What's his response? (v15–17, 21)

◉ Read verses 22–29

ⓓ Who else does this psalm remind us of? (v22, 26)

This psalm seems to be written by a king who God rescued from his enemies. But it also reminds us of the perfect King sent by God. Jesus even quoted v22 about Himself. People rejected Him, yet God used Him to miraculously rescue sinners. It's Jesus who emerges from the background of this great psalm. It's Him you should praise and thank right now.

PRAY ABOUT IT

Use Psalm 118 as the starting point for your prayers today.

→ TAKE IT FURTHER

More background info on page 125.

TAKE IT FURTHER

If you want a little more at the end of each day's study, this is where you come. The TAKE IT FURTHER sections give you something extra. They look at some of the issues covered in the day's study, pose deeper questions, and point you to the big picture of the whole Bible.

EZEKIEL
Know God, know hope

1 – TELL A VISION

Here's how Ezekiel fits together:

Chs 1–24: No hope
God's people rejected God. His judgment on them would be as severe as it was unstoppable. So no point clinging to false hopes that it would be any different.

Chs 25–32: Still no hope
The nations around Israel were to face God's judgment too — for the way they'd trashed God's people and mocked God.

Chs 33–48: Know hope
Could there be a future for God's people after His judgment? Incredibly, yes, as God stood by His promises and acted in line with His perfect character. Only in God would His people find solid, substantial hope for the future. We'll see how this Old Testament book points us to the future and helps us understand more about Jesus and the hope He holds out to us.

2 – MISSION IMPOSSIBLE?
Read Ezekiel 3 v 11 & 17

Ezekiel was to proclaim God's warnings to people he knew and liked; people he'd been exiled with and lived among. See the massive responsibility he was given (v17–18)? God's people now (Christians) also have the same job of taking God's words to a lost generation.

▶ *Why is it vital that we do that?*

3 – SIEGE MENTALITY
Read John 6 v 35–40

▶ *How does Jesus compare Himself to hunger-satisfying bread? (v35)*

▶ *How do we get hold of this life-giving bread? (v35, 37, 40)*

▶ *Is it down to us, or is someone else behind this amazing gift? (v37–40)*

All this talk of bread has left people hungry. But Jesus can satisfy real hunger — our hunger for life, for a reason to live. It's not down to us at all, it's a gift from God. All we have to do is **believe** that only Jesus can satisfy our cravings.

4 – HAIRY STORY

HIstory time! Chapters 4 and 5 of Ezekiel happened in 593BC, five years after the first siege of Jerusalem by Nebuchadnezzar and the Babylonians. The people of Judah and its capital, Jerusalem, now lived in fear of the Babylonians. Many of them had even been taken away to Babylon.

Four years after Ezekiel made his model, the Babylonians invaded Judah and destroyed most of its towns and cities. Jerusalem was under siege. After a while, the people of Jerusalem were rescued by Egypt. But the people continued to sin against God and in 587BC the city finally fell and was systematically destroyed. It was this horrible future that Ezekiel was revealing to God's people.

5 –IDOL SPECULATION
Read Ezekiel 6 v 3–7

"High places" were mostly shrines that existed when the Israelites took over the land. At first, they were harmless enough (Samuel and Solomon both used them to worship God, see 1 Samuel 9 v 14, 1 Kings 3 v 2–4). But once God's temple was built in Jerusalem, formal worship at these places was banned. Two kings, Hezekiah and Josiah, tried to wipe out the high places (2 Kings 18 v 4; 23 v 19) but with little long-term effect.

▶ *Which phrase is repeated in Ezekiel 6 v 7, 10, 13, 14?*

This phrase is repeated over 60 times in Ezekiel, so it must be vital to us understanding this book. God was acting to ensure His people knew Him as He is — the one true God — and knew what He was like. Do you live with that awareness?

6 – IDOL TALK

The four actions in God's temple (worshipping idols, animals and the sun) show how low Jerusalem had sunk. They had made religion more important than God. And that's still a danger today. But, astonishingly, God's presence was still there. He'd stay until the very last moment of their rejection of Him.

▶ *How might you put religion or tradition ahead of God?*
▶ *What can you do about it?*

7 – GOD'S GONE

God's presence is His most treasured gift. It's at the heart of what He promises to His people.

Read Psalm 34 v 7–14

▶ *What is promised to those who fear God?*
▶ *What do people who fear God avoid?*
▶ *And what do they pursue?*

9 – A BIG BREAKTHROUGH

Read 2 Peter 3 v 3–14

▶ *How were people mocking Christianity in Peter's day? (v4)*
▶ *What had these people forgotten? (v5–6)*
▶ *What will happen when Jesus does come again? (v7)*
▶ *How does God view time differently to us? (v8)*
▶ *What will definitely happen one day? (v10)*
▶ *So what should our attitude be? (v11–13)*
▶ *And what should we do? (v11, 14)*

10 – PROPHET AND LOSS
Read Ezekiel 13 v 22–23
Faithful preacher that Ezekiel was, he pronounced God's judgment on the frauds, liars and exploiters of his day. Especially the ones who claimed to be religious and on God's side. This made Ezekiel deeply unpopular. Those who tell lies about the future can expect, one day, to find the future has caught up with them. God's Day is coming and then His power will be seen as an unstoppable force to be reckoned with. *"Then you will know that I am the Lord"* (v23).

JAMES
Fantastic faith

11 – JAMES ON TRIAL
**Read verse 2 again
and then Philippians 1 v 6**
Somebody famous said: "Man's destroyed, not by suffering, but by suffering without meaning". The Bible never belittles hurt. And it gives us a way to understand it: that God's able to use it in the process of making us more like Jesus.
▶ *How does pain and hurt wake us up to God?*
▶ *How have you seen this to be true in your life?*

12 – CASH OR CROWN?
Read 1 Corinthians 9 v 24–27
▶ *What do believers need to do? (v24–25)*
▶ *What's the great reward? (v25)*

▶ *How did Paul's lifestyle help him with his mission? (v26–27)*

13 – TEMPTING TIMES
Read verse 13 again
God can't be tempted and He tempts no one — His motives are always good. The Greek word for trials and for temptations is the same. God uses hard times as trials for us, but Satan uses them to cause us to doubt God. Watch out!

Read verse 18
"Firstfruits": in Old Testament times, the first and best crops were set aside to thank God for keeping His promises. Christians are like firstfruits — our new birth shows God is faithful and that we're "reserved" for God, out of all His creation! God chose us way before we decided on Him.

14 – LISTEN UP
It's not always wrong to get angry (though see Paul's warnings in Ephesians 4 v 26–27). There is righteous anger — a sense of moral outrage at sin and its effects. God gets angry, but His anger is controlled and settled.
▶ *In contrast, what's our anger normally like?*

Here's a great verse to learn by heart:
Proverbs 10 v 19

15 – MIRROR MIRROR ON THE WALL
Read verse 25 again
How can law and freedom go together? Doesn't following God's law take away

111

your freedom? Well, we could choose to ignore the dentist's orders and not brush our teeth. We're free to do so. But we know the end result would be decay and pain. See the point? Get away from thinking that living God's way will cramp your style or make life boring. Obeying God frees us from slavery to sin.

Check out John 8 v 31–32

16 – RELIGIOUS EDUCATION
Read 1 John 2 v 15–17
Worldliness is when we care more for our comforts than others' survival. If we chase promotion, prestige and possessions more than putting God and others first, then we've failed to keep ourselves from being polluted by the world. And we place a large question mark over our religion.

Read Romans 12 v 1–8
- ▶ *What should believers do? (v1)*
- ▶ *What should they no longer do? (v2)*
- ▶ *How are we transformed? (v2)*
- ▶ *What will the end result be? (v2)*
- ▶ *What does this mean in practice with other Christians? (v3–8)*

17 – FIRM FAVOURITES
Ever heard it said: "To get going as a church / youth group, we need good people and someone with plenty of money"? Or: "What we need is for a sports star / tv star / royalty to become a Christian".
- ▶ *What would James say is wrong with such attitudes?*

Read Philippians 2 v 5–11
- ▶ *What attitudes and ambitions do you need to change?*

18 – MERCY SIDE
Read verse 12 again
A law giving freedom — the gospel shows God's demands but gives us the power to obey them. To get us started, God forgives us. To help us keep going, He gives us His Holy Spirit.

19 – FAITH IN ACTION
Is James disagreeing with the apostle Paul? James says "You're not saved by faith alone" (v24). Paul says: "You're saved by faith, not by works (good deeds)" (Ephesians 2 v 8–9). They're not disagreeing, but writing with different purposes. James says our belief in Jesus must result in good works; Paul says our good works won't earn a rescue for heaven in the first place.

20 – TONGUE TWISTING
Read Proverbs 15 v 1–7
- ▶ *How should we respond in an argument? (v1)*
- ▶ *How shouldn't we? (v1)*
- ▶ *How can we use our words positively? (v2, 4, 7)*
- ▶ *And negatively? (v2, 4)*
- ▶ *What do we need to remember? (v3)*
- ▶ *What do you specifically need to work on, words-wise?*

21 – WISE UP

Re-read verse 18

"A harvest of righteousness" probably means a group of people focused on obeying God and caring for each other. What a church that would be!

▶ *Do you seek to serve/please/glorify God or yourself?*

22 – RESISTANCE IS FERTILE

Read verse 4 again

"Adulterous people" is a common Bible term for people who've betrayed their promises and turned from God. We can't be a friend of God and a friend of the world — behaving as a society that rejects God behaves. Yet we keep living as if we can.

Read 2 Corinthians 6 v 14 – 7 v 1

▶ *How will this work out for you in everyday situations?*

23 – WHO'S THE JUDGE?

Read verses 11–12 again and answer:

▶ *How do I view other Christians I know? As brothers and sisters or as nuisances and enemies?*

▶ *How do I view God's law? Am I too big to obey it?*

▶ *How do I view God? Weak and irrelevant or as He really is?*

▶ *How do I view myself? Above everyone else?*

The right response to the failings of others is not criticism and gossip but prayer and encouragement.

▶ *Who do you need to change your*

attitude about?

▶ *How will you stop yourself slandering them from now on?*

24 – RICH PICKINGS

Read Amos 4 v 1–3

▶ *What did these women do wrong?*

▶ *What would happen to them?*

Amos compared these wealthy women to the best cows: well-fed, spoiled. They mistreated the poor and needy, caring more about what they were drinking.

▶ *How do you treat the poor and needy?*

▶ *What positive things can you do for someone worse off than you?*

25 – WAIT FOR IT

Read Matthew 5 v 33–37

▶ *What rule did the Pharisees and teachers of the law teach? (v33)*

▶ *How is Jesus' command more demanding? (v37)*

▶ *Have you ever been guilty of breaking the Pharisees' rule?*

▶ *What about Jesus' command?*

Are you a man/woman of your word? Do you keep your promises? Can people trust you when you say you'll do something?

26 – SURVIVAL GUIDE

For Elijah's story, read 1 Kings 17 v 1–6 and then 1 Kings 18 v 1–2 and 16–46.

27 – DON'T JUST STAND THERE!

Well done for reaching the end of James. Are you exhausted? Has God changed you at all? Is there anything you decided to do that you've not done yet? Take time to read through the whole letter, talking to God as you go along.

EZEKIEL

28 – KNOW GOD, KNOW HOPE

Read Ezekiel 15 v 1–8

God compared His people to the useless part of a vine, only fit to be used as fire wood. That's how charred and useless Jerusalem was after rebelling against God and being attacked by the Babylonians. And soon, the Babylonians would return to finish off the job.

Read John 15 v 1–8

▷ What was Jesus' big claim? (v1)
▷ What does God do with bad branches? (v2)
▷ And with good ones?
▷ What do you think it means to "remain" in Jesus? (v4)
▷ What's the promise if we do? (v5, 7)

Unlike Israel, Jesus is the *true vine*. Christians are the branches — they have a close relationship with Him. Tragically, people who don't live God's way, bearing fruit for Him, will be cut off from God. But those who do serve Him, He'll make even more fruitful.

A branch only produces grapes when

it's connected to the vine. We must stay connected to Jesus. We need to take in Jesus' words and live by them (v7). He'll help us to bear fruit if we ask Him (v7). And if we serve Him, then people will know we're His disciples and God will get the glory (v8).

29 – TALL TREE TALE

In chapters 15–17, we've read three stories — about a vine, a prostitute, and two eagles. All three show how horribly rebellious Judah was to God. And how God would use Babylon to punish Judah, less than 5 years into the future. God's people had broken their covenant agreement with Him. They'd chosen themselves and this world over living for God. They'd turned their back on God and would have to face the consequences. The same is still true for people today.

Yet, in the middle of all this talk of God's judgment on His people, Ezekiel keeps mentioning a "remnant" who God would bring back to His city, Jerusalem. And Ezekiel points us further into the future, to Jesus and the perfect kingdom He'll bring. Despite all Ezekiel's warnings, he reminds us that God's true people (Christians) have a bright and safe future ahead of them!

30 – SOUR GRAPES

Read Ezekiel 19 v 1–14

Chapter 19 is a sad song about Judah and three of its kings. The lioness (v2) = the nation of Judah. The first strong lion (v3–4) = King Jehoahaz (2 Kings 23 v 33).

He was vicious and cruel but the Egyptians captured him. The next strong lion (v5–9) is probably King Jehoiachin (2 Kings 24 v 8–15). He met a similar fate. Verses 10–14 probably refer to King Zedekiah's reign (2 Kings 24 v 18 – 25 v 7). None of these kings turned to God for help, and had to face the disastrous consequences.

The exiles blamed their situation on the sins of others and didn't take responsibility for their own wrongs. They looked to powerful nations to rescue them, instead of crying out to God. Before we can be made right with God, we need to realise that we're sinners and deserve God's punishment. And to know that only Jesus can rescue us.

31 – HISTORY MYSTERY
Read Ezekiel 20 v 45–49
A forest fire is heading south. Babylon attacked Judah from the north, heading south. God sent the Babylonians to punish His rebellious people. We've already seen why. Someone once said that history is "His story". God is in charge. He's in control. Of history. Of the world. Of everything. We must never forget that, whatever is happening in the world.

32 – SINFUL SISTERS
If you have time, **read Ezekiel chapters 21 and 22.** Here's how a Bible boffin sums up these chapters: "A fire is said to sweep through the land (end of chapter 20). The fire becomes a sword in the hands of King Nebuchadnezzar of Babylon. He has come to fight against Israel. God used him to

punish the Israelites.

"But God promises His people a glorious future. The church continues to grow despite all Satan throws in its path. But the end of the wicked is sure too — total destruction. There is no hope for those who remain God's enemies. Without turning back to God, the sword hangs over their heads!"
(*God Strengthens* by Derek Thomas)

33 – DEVASTATING NEWS
So why did God do such a seemingly cruel thing to Ezekiel and his wife? The deliberate death of a young woman seems outrageously cruel. We need to remember that God takes no pleasure in the death of anyone, even the wicked (Ezekiel 18 v 32). God took no pleasure in this act; in fact it probably caused Him much grief.

What justified it in God's eyes was its value as a sign. We have to assume it achieved its purpose and pointed at least some people towards acceptance, confession, repentance and salvation. If some exiles turned back to God and found saving grace and life in the wake of that terrible incident, then her death was not in vain. Remember that God Himself would give His one and only Son to death to rescue sinners like us (from *The Message of Ezekiel* by Chris Wright).

34 – CONDEMN NATIONS
Time for some historical research. For **Ammon**'s conflicts with Israel, check out Judges 10 & 11; 1 Samuel 11;

2 Samuel 10; 2 Kings 24.
For **Moab**, see Numbers 22–24.
Edom info is in Genesis 25 v 23;
Psalm 137 v 7; Obadiah v 1–21;
Malachi 1 v 3–5.
And **Philistine** phacts are in 1 Samuel 17
and 2 Samuel 5 v 17–25.

35 –TYRE PUNCTURED
Skim read Ezekiel chapter 27
▶ *How is Tyre compared to a great ship?*
  (v4–11)
▶ *How was Tyre at trading? (v12–25)*
▶ *How did Tyre view itself? (v3)*
▶ *What would happen to its wealth?*
  (v27)
▶ *What's the news for people who rely*
  on themselves and chase money?
▶ *What does God say to people who*
  worship business or their career?
Read Proverbs 28 v 6, 11, 20, 22

36 – THE END FOR EGYPT
Read Ezekiel 30 v 1–19
The focus of this chapter is North Africa:
Egypt, Cush (Ethiopia), Put (Libya) and
Lydia (not sure where that is). "The day
of the Lord" is mentioned (v3). This often
refers to God's final day of judgment, but
can also refer to specific events such as
God's punishment of these nations. For
these countries, a storm is gathering (v3)
— God's anger is about to be unleashed
on His enemies. They would be punished
for worshipping fake gods (v13). God's
day of judgment was inescapable for these
nations. And when Jesus returns as Judge,
it will be completely unavoidable.

Read verses 20–26
Some of God's people were still relying on
Pharaoh and the Egyptians to rescue them
from the Babylonians. Bad move. God was
against Egypt (v22) so they didn't stand
a chance. This Pharaoh (Hophra) was
defeated in war and then assassinated by
his own people. God's in complete control
and His enemies will not win.

MATTHEW
Are you ready?
38 – ROTTEN RELIGION
▶ *What was one of Jesus' criticisms of*
  the religious leaders? (end of v3)?
▶ *What did Jesus tell His own followers*
  to do? (v11–12)

Read Philippians 2 v 5-11
▶ *How did Jesus practise what He*
  preached?
▶ *How did He humble Himself?*
▶ *How was He exalted?*
▶ *How does this give us inspiration to*
  humble ourselves, and confidence
  we'll be exalted?

39 – PULLING NO PUNCHES
Re-read verses 16–22
▶ *What were the religious leaders*
  saying? (v16–20)
This sounds strange to us! But Jesus
is saying that the Jewish leaders are
completely missing what really matters.
The gold is only worth anything because
it's in the temple (v17)… and the temple
is only worth anything because of who

lives in it (ie: God, v21). True religion is not about making up rules and nitpicking little details: it's about "God's throne and … the one who sits on it" (v22).

🔹 *What dominates your religion? Making and keeping rules, or knowing and serving the Ruler?*

40 – GOOD LOOKS

Three thousand years ago, God decided to choose a man to be king of His nation, Israel. He sent His messenger, the prophet Samuel, to go and find this man.

Read 1 Samuel 16 v 1–13

🔹 *Who did Samuel think God would choose? (v6)*

🔹 *Who did God choose? (v12–13)*

🔹 *What did Samuel need to learn? (v7)*

🔹 *Outward appearance, or the heart — what do you care about most: in your view of yourself? in your view of others?*

41 – JESUS' WINGS

In Matthew 23 v 35, Jesus talks about the blood of righteous Abel.

Read Genesis 4 v 2–8

Abel gives to God the very best he has (v4); Cain brought a few things he could spare (v3).

🔹 *How does God respond to the two brothers? (v4–5)*

🔹 *How does Cain react? (v5, 8)*

Just like the religious leaders, Cain kills someone who is showing him how to worship and love God, instead of listening

to him. We may not kill those who are more wholehearted in their faith: but do we sometimes envy them, or find reasons to look down on them or criticise them, or simply refuse to have anything to do with them?

42 – THE END OF THE WORLD

It's actually kind of nice to show us how hard it will be to live in this world as a Christian. It means it won't surprise us! But is it worth it?

Read Revelation 7 v 13–17

This is a vision of our eternal future. And the people there have "come out of the great tribulation" — in other words, have kept their faith despite the difficulties of the Christian life.

🔹 *What in these verses shows it's worth continuing to trust "in the blood of the Lamb", in Jesus' death?*

43 – WHERE'S THE WORLD HEADING?

Read Daniel 7 v 13–14

🔹 *What happens to the "one like a son of man"?*

🔹 *What is He given?*

Jesus often refers to Himself as the "Son of Man". It's a way of Him saying "I" or "me" — but Daniel 7 shows us it's much more than that. Jesus is the Son of Man, who will one day rule over everything for all time. We need to remember that Jesus is not just our friend, our brother, our helper — He is the most powerful, awesome man in the universe.

44 – AND THEN BANG

Read 1 Thessalonians 4 v 15 – 5 v 3

▷ What links 5 v 2 with Matthew 24 v 43?

▷ What particularly excites you in this passage?

▷ What is the application? (4 v 18)

▷ How can you do that this week?

45 – DON'T BE F-OIL-ISH

Jesus' parable here doesn't mean we shouldn't share your faith with others!

Read 1 Peter 3 v 15

To use Jesus' parable, we can't give other people our oil, or faith in Jesus. But we can tell them to get their own before it's too late. And we can pray that God will make them see that they need Jesus more than anything else. Why not pray for a non-Christian friend right now? And then look for a chance to talk to them about your faith and your future.

46 – NO TIME TO RELAX

Read Romans 12 v 4–13

This is a list of some of the talents — circumstances and abilities — Jesus gives His people to serve Him with.

▷ What does v5 remind us about our relationship with our church?

▷ Which of these talents have you got?

▷ Are you using them to serve Jesus and His people?

▷ How can you do that more?

47 – BE SHEEPISH

Read Philippians 2 v 9–11

▷ One day, when He returns, what will everyone do?

The question isn't whether someone will say, and mean: "Jesus is King", but when. Will it be now, so that Jesus' return is terrific news for them? Or will it be on the day He comes, when His return will be terrifying for them?

▷ How are these verses exciting?

▷ How are they challenging?

48 – BEAUTY IN THE DARKNESS

Re-read 26 v 1–5

▷ What are the religious elite wanting to do? (v4)

▷ But what has Jesus already said will happen? (v2)

As Jesus faces arrest, trial and execution, it will look as if the leaders are in charge. But they're not! Fact is, Jesus is in charge — He is only killed because He allows Himself to be. As we go on through Matthew, we need to remember that appearances are deceptive. The ones who look as though they are powerful are weak. The One who seems weak is in full control — even as He dies.

▷ How does this make you feel about Jesus?

▷ How does this encourage you in your Christian life?

49 – PASSOVER PICTURE

Read 1 Corinthians 11 v 23–28

▷ What else does this passage tell us about how we approach Communion?

50 – SCATTERED
Read Matthew 28 v 16–20

▷ *How does this episode link back to today's passage?*

▷ *How does it give you great confidence that what Jesus says will happen, does actually happen?*

EZEKIEL

51 – KNOW GOD, KNOW HOPE
Read verses 12–20

So, we're individually responsible to God. Ezekiel has told his hearers already that rebels would have no part in the return (20 v 35–38). So verse 13 is a warning that trusting in ourselves or our past behaviour is never the same as trusting God.

52 – THE BAD SHEPHERDS
Read Jeremiah 23 v 1–6

▷ *What had the leaders of God's people been doing? (v1–2)*

▷ *So what would God do? (v2)*

▷ *What's the great news for God's people in the future? (v3–4)*

▷ *How will this King rule His people? (v5)*

▷ *What will He be called? (v6)*

▷ *What will happen to God's chosen people? (v6)*

There was no hope of God removing His judgment. But there was hope of a future *after* God's judgment. He would rescue them again and give them a perfect King to rule them. The New Testament tells us this King is Jesus.

53 – THE GOOD SHEPHERD
Read John 10 v 11–21

Jesus said He came to give us "life to the full".

▷ *What would it cost for Him to give us this life? (v11, 15)*

Jesus wasn't pushed into it. He voluntarily gave up His life for people who needed His rescue. You and me. Not only would Jesus give His life to rescue sinners like us, He'd be raised back to life to beat death.

The Jews thought that only they would go to live with God forever. But Jesus dropped a bombshell — He had come to save non–Jewish people too (v16). They would all be one flock — one big family. And we can see this incredibly diverse family all around us; people from every nation, language and background, all worshipping Jesus.

54 – A NEW HEART
**Read Ezekiel 36 v 25–27
then Romans 8 v 9–17**

▷ *Who's in control of Christians? (v9)*

▷ *What does Paul call Christians? (v16)*

▷ *So how should we live? (v12–13)*

▷ *What do Christians share in with Jesus? (v17)*

All Christians have the Holy Spirit in them, helping them live God's way. God's Spirit raised Jesus from death and He will also give new life to Christians. Their bodies will die but they will go on to live with God for ever.

Christians are God's children. That means they have to stop being ruled by sin (v12). Christians are also God's heirs, along with His Son, Jesus. The inheritance has an up side and a down side. Christians will share in Christ's sufferings — they will be persecuted for serving God. But they will also share in God's glory — they will one day live with Him and see what He's really like. Phenomenal.

56 – GOG SMACKED

Read Revelation 20 v 7–10

▷ *Who is behind opposition to God and His people? (v7)*

▷ *What's the great news for God's people? (v9–10)*

▷ *Who's in complete control?*

57 – TEMPLE VISION

Chapter 42 gives a very complicated description of the priests' rooms in the temple. Read it, if you dare. It also shows how perfect and symmetrical God's plans were (v16–20). Everything about God's plan for His people's future worship is perfect. In fact, the whole function of this elaborately designed building was to aid the worship of God. God longs to be with His people. And we should long to be with Him and to worship Him with the way we live our lives.

59 – YOUR HOLINESS

Read verses 10–14 again

The Levites had three main duties: guarding the temple; killing and cooking sacrifices; and helping the worshippers in their worship. These were not even top tasks (the best jobs were reserved for Aaron's descendants). But these Levites had still been seriously irresponsible in the past, even allowing idol worship in God's temple. Because of this, their temple tasks were reduced.

People who work for God's church are accountable to God. As Jesus put it: *"From everyone who has been given much, much will be demanded; and from the one who has been entrusted with much, much more will be asked."* (Luke 12 v 48)

60 – LAND AND SACRIFICE

Read Ezekiel 45 v 9–12

Even in this newlook Jerusalem, there is the possibility of sin — false measures and weights. This shows that Ezekiel's vision isn't of heaven but of Jerusalem in New Testament times. God's people (Christians) must be characterised by honesty. Cheating may bring short-term profit, but God sees all and won't tolerate it. This was a favourite topic of God's prophets (Amos 8 v 5; Micah 6 v 10–12).

61 – LET IT FLOW

Check out the New Testament fulfilment of Ezekiel 47 & 48:

John 2 v 18–22: All that the temple stood for was realised in Jesus. In Him, God was present among His people.
John 7 v 3–39: The temple has been built and is being built.
Revelation 21 & 22: The symbol gives

way to reality!

That's it. Ezekiel's done. Well done for surviving! Know God, know hope. The gospel says "No" to all the hopes people manufacture. There's only one place to put your hope — and that's in God and His promises. Go with **1 Peter 1 v 3**.

62 – PRAISE THE LORD!

**Read verse 10 again,
then Job 28 v 20–28**

▶ *Is it easy to find true wisdom and understanding? (v21)*

▶ *Who knows where to find it? (v23)*

▶ *How would you define wisdom and understanding in your own words, based on v28?*

ESTHER
God's beauty queen

63 – VASHTI VANISHES

Read these proverbs and memorise the one that really speaks to you.

Proverbs 29 v 11
Proverbs 14 v 17
Proverbs 15 v 18
Proverbs 20 v 1
Proverbs 23 v 20–21
Proverbs 31 v 4–5

64 – WHAT A BEAUTY!

Why isn't God mentioned in Esther? Well, think about...
a) the book's readers: written for Jews in Persia. Any Jew who trusted God would see His hand in the events described.
b) the book's enemies: maybe the book could have been destroyed if it rubbished the Persian emperor and his religion.
c) the books contents: God isn't absent here (eg: true fasting, mentioned in 4 v 16, always included prayer to God.
d) the book's purpose: written to record the Jews' rescue under Xerxes and to ensure the Purim festival (chapter 9) was kept.

So, although they were miles from Jerusalem, they'd be sustained by the reminder in the book of Esther that God was still looking after His people. Even when God seems absent, He's not. He's always at work, behind the scenes.

65 – THE PLOT THICKENS

Life for the Jews in exile seemed great. They had a fairly comfortable life, and now one of their own was queen and another had rescued the king. It seemed as if they were safe and secure. But that quickly changed due to Haman's personal grudge against Mordecai. Suddenly all Jews were staring death in the face.

That's the truth of life for God's people. It's sometimes easy to cruise along in life, assuming everything's alright. But God hasn't promised us an easy life. His people WILL be persecuted from time to time and we have to expect it and make sure we trust God and stick with Him when it happens. Because we know that we have a secure and wonderful future with Him.

66 – GETTING THE SACK(CLOTH)

Read verses 12–14 again

"Deliverance will arise from another place". Despite the looming crisis, Mordecai trusted that God keeps His promises. Whatever response God's people make to Him, God achieves His purposes.

"You've come to royal position for such a time". It's no coincidence. God had arranged events to put Esther in place as queen for this big moment. This is God's providence. By providence, we mean: God's action to benefit His people — through all circumstances and human decisions, good and bad.

68 – ROBE REVERSAL

Esther chapter 6 is about reversal — hope and dashed hopes. And it's about the providential work of God. There are more "coincidences" in this chapter than any other. So many that it can't be down to chance. Re-read the chapter and see if you can spot them all. Things were looking very bad for God's people, the Jews. But these coincidences bring a glimmer of hope into this desperate situation. God will work all things for good in the end.

69 – THE BIG BANQUET

God made sure that Esther became queen so she could act to rescue His people. Incredible. So that means...
the dismissal of Vashti (1 v 19),
the choosing of Esther by Hegai (2 v 9),
Mordecai's overhearing of the assassination plot (2 v 23),

the roll of the dice (3 v 7),
Haman's building of the gallows (5 v 14)
Xerxes' sleepless night (6 v 1)...
were all arranged by God to benefit His people. Awesome!

70 – CELEBRATION NATION

Esther chapter 8 is very similar to chapter 3, but with some significant differences.
- How have Mordecai's fortunes changed?
- How have things turned around for the Jews?
- Who do you think was behind it all?
- What evidence is there?

71 – DAY OF DESTRUCTION

According to the Bible, God's plan is to draw together a bunch of people, from across the world, who trust in His Son Jesus. Esther shows God overseeing our freely-made decisions (including our sin and our stupidity) to achieve that purpose. He's not caught out by a drunk Xerxes, a hesitant Esther, a murderous Haman, a stubborn Mordecai or a very enthusiastic people. Nothing can stop God's plans.

72 – PARTY!

Read Esther 4 v 12–16

Take the Esther challenge. The Lord put Esther in that particular situation for His special task (v14). She worried, then prayed... then set herself to do God's will, whatever the outcome (v16).
- Will you do the same in the situation God's placed you?
- What exactly will that mean for you?

PSALMS

73 – THE GOOD LIFE
Read Philippians 4 v 4–9
▶ What tips are given for living a
   godly life?
   v4:
   v5:
   v6:
   v8:
▶ Which of these do you need to put
   into practice?
▶ How will you do it?
▶ What's the promise if we live like
   this? (v7, 9)

74 – GLORY TO GOD
Read verses 7–9 again and then
1 Samuel 1 v 1 – 2 v 11 to see God
in action.

75 – TIME TO TREMBLE
For the background to this psalm,
check out **Exodus 14; 17; Numbers 20;
Joshua 3 – 4**.

MATTHEW

76 – ARE YOU READY?
Read Jeremiah 25 v 15–29
▶ What do we learn about "the cup"?
   (v15–16)
▶ Who has to drink from it? (v17–27)
▶ Does there seem any possibility of
   escape? (v28–29)
▶ When we remember this is the cup
   God gave Jesus instead of the nations,
   how should we respond?

77 – WHO'S IN CONTROL?
Read 1 Peter 2 v 18–25
▶ How does Peter tell us to respond to
   being badly treated? (v18–20)
▶ Why have Christians been "called"
   to this? (v21)
▶ What is the example Jesus set?
   (v22–24)

78 – WHO'S ON TRIAL?
Re-read verses 63–66
Because of the claims He makes, Jesus
doesn't leave His judges, or us, with the
option of thinking He's a "nice guy" or a
"wise teacher". Because He claims to be
"the Christ, the Son of God", we have
only two options: to say He's telling the
truth, or to say He's a complete fraud.
The high priest took the second option:
Christians take the first.
▶ Do your friends know that Jesus is
   either the God who will judge them,
   or He is a complete fake?
▶ How could you challenge them as
   to which option they take?

79 – DENIED
Read John 21 v 15–19
▶ What does Jesus ask Simon Peter?
▶ Why do you think He asks Him
   three times?
▶ What job does He give Peter? (v17)
▶ How will Peter die? (v18–19)
This was actually wonderful news for
Peter. He had denied Jesus was facing
death, but Jesus says Peter would be able
to stay loyal to his Lord even when Peter
was facing his own death!

80 – DEAD END OR HAPPY END?

In Matthew 27 v 9, Matthew quotes from the prophet Jeremiah, and also from Zechariah.

Read Zechariah 11 v 8b–13

Zechariah was God's chosen leader of His people — but they detested him (v8). So in v12, he basically says: what price do you put on God's plan for me to lead you?

▶ How much do they give him? (v12)

Same as Judas! Both the people here, and Judas with Jesus, are putting a price on God's head, deciding how much He's worth. For 30 pieces of silver, Judas is prepared to turn his back on Jesus.

▶ What do you turn your back on Jesus for?

▶ What are you saying at that point about how much He's worth to you?

▶ What do you need to change?

81 – GOD'S KING? KILL HIM!

Re-read verses 27-31

How do these verses make you feel? These soldiers are laughing at the idea that Jesus is a king. It's easy to think: I'd never do that! But whenever we sin, we're basically laughing at the thought that Jesus should be in charge of our lives.

82 – LOSER OR LORD

Read verse 32 again and then Matthew 16 v 24–25

▶ How is Simon a picture of what it means to be a real Christian?

We won't carry Jesus' cross today. But Jesus says that we are to die to what is easiest or feels best to us, and give up living for ourselves.

▶ How are you doing that?

▶ How could you do that more?

83 – THE BIG QUESTION

On the cross, Jesus was quoting the first words of Psalm 22, written a thousand years before…

Read Psalm 22 v 1–18

▶ How do these verses help us understand what Jesus went through on the cross? (v1-2, 6-8, 14-18)

▶ In Matthew, how did we see v7-8, v15 and v18 coming true for Jesus?

▶ Jesus went through all this for you to be forgiven, if you're His follower. How does this make you feel?

84 – CAN PEOPLE LIVE WITH GOD?

Re-read verses 51-53

This sounds bizarre! But it's a fantastic visual aid showing us what Jesus' death and resurrection mean. Anyone who dies as a "holy" person — someone who has known and trusted God — is given new life beyond the grave by Jesus' death and resurrection. If you're a Christian, you will be, too! And the "holy city" (v53) won't be the city of Jerusalem in Israel — it'll be the city of Jerusalem in God's perfect new world (see Revelation 21 v 1-5).

86 – JESUS IS RISEN – SO WHAT?

One of the great messages of the resurrection is that it proves that what Jesus promises always comes true.

Read Matthew 10 v 39; 11 v 28-30; 12 v 50; 19 v 28-29; 24 v 44; 28 v 20.
We know that these will all come true, just as His promise to rise from the dead did. Which of these promises particularly excites you today?

87 – KILLING THE TRUTH
Read 1 Corinthians 15 v 13–19
🔽 *Why does whether or not Jesus rose from the dead matter?*

Read verse 20
This verse is brilliant! Jesus has risen! Let that put a smile on your face today, whatever else happens!

88 – WHAT JESUS DESERVES
Read Genesis 12 v 1–3
God promised Abraham (known here as Abram) that through one of his descendants, people from every nation would know the blessing of knowing God (v3). Jesus is that descendant. Through His death and resurrection, He offers everyone the opportunity to be blessed by God. And Matthew 28 v 19 shows the way God's blessing (promised to Abraham and offered through Jesus) is taken to people. It's by us!
🔽 *How does this excite you about telling people about Jesus?*
🔽 *So who will you talk to?*

89 – WHY WORSHIP?
Now it's time for you to answer the original question again.
🔽 *Why do you worship God?*
If it's still hard to answer, read through Psalm 115, picking out all the reasons God deserves our respect and praise.

90 – A PASSIONATE LIFE
Read Romans 12 v 1–8
🔽 *What does Paul want the Roman Christians to do? (v1)*
🔽 *How are we transformed? (v2)*
🔽 *What will the end result be? (v2)*
🔽 *What does this mean in practice with other Christians? (v3–8)*
Paul says Christians should give their whole lives over to God. That means pleasing God in everything we do, say and think about. And the place to start showing our thanks to God is among His people — using our God-given abilities to serve Him and other Christians.

91 – SHORT AND SWEET
Questions to ponder and pray about:
🔽 *What have I got to be thankful for?*
🔽 *How can I be more aware of what God does and has done for me?*
🔽 *How do I need His help to tell my friends about gospel truth?*

92 – IN THE BACKGROUND
For the big picture of this psalm...
Read verse 22, then Luke 20 v 9–19 and Acts 4 v 8–12.
Read Psalm 118 v 25–26, followed by John 12 v 12–16.

RSVP

engage wants to hear from YOU!

▶ Share experiences of God at work in your life
▶ Any questions you have about the Bible or the Christian life?
▶ How can we make *engage* better?

Email us — **martin@thegoodbook.co.uk**

Or send us a letter/postcard/cartoon/cheesecake to:
**engage, B1, Blenheim House, Longmead Business Park,
Epsom, Surrey, KT19 9AP, UK**

In the next **engage**

Job Why me?
Mark All about Jesus
Proverbs Wise up!
Galatians Free for all
Malachi The return
Plus: Relationships
Active church
Does prayer really work?
Toolbox & Real Lives

Order **engage** now!

Make sure you order the next issue of **engage**. Or even better, grab a one-year s ubscription to make sure **engage** lands in your hands as soon as it's out.

Call us to order in the UK on 0333 123 0880
International: +44 (0) 20 8942 0880

or visit your friendly neighbourhood website:
UK: www.thegoodbook.co.uk
N America: www.thegoodbook.com
Australia: www.thegoodbook.com.au
New Zealand: www.thegoodbook.co.nz